Europe as I See It

Europe as I See It

Romano Prodi

Translated by Allan Cameron

Polity

First published in Italian as *Un'idea dell'Europa*
© 1999 by Società editrice il Mulino, Bologna.

First published in 2000 by Polity Press in association
with Blackwell Publishers Ltd.

Published with the assistance of the French Ministry of Culture.

Editorial office:
Polity Press
65 Bridge Street
Cambridge CB2 1UR, UK

Marketing and production:
Blackwell Publishers Ltd
108 Cowley Road
Oxford OX4 1JF, UK

Published in the USA by
Blackwell Publishers Inc.
350 Main Street
Malden, MA 02148, USA

A catalogue record for this book is available from the British Library.
Prodi, Romano.
[Idea dell'Europa. English]
Europe as I see it / Romano Prodi ; translated by Allan Cameron.
p. cm.
ISBN 0-7456-2496-0—ISBN 0-7456-2497-9 (pbk.)
1. European Union. 2. European Union—Italy. 3. Competition,
International. 4. International economic relations. I. Title.
HC240.P74613 2000
337.1'42—dc21   00-037480

Typeset in 11 on 13pt Berling
by Graphicraft Limited, Hong Kong
Printed in Great Britain by TJ International, Padstow, Cornwall

This book is printed on acid-free paper.

Contents

Introduction

Europe at the turn of the millennium finds itself at a cross-roads. On the one hand, a bright future is promised by completion of monetary union, the opportunity to make the old international barriers a thing of the past by enlarging the European Union and NATO, and the universal affirmation of the principles of liberty and democracy. But, on the other hand, there are increasing anxieties over falling populations, mass immigration and doubts over the possibility of maintaining the European model of social welfare. Unsustainable levels of both structural and cyclical unemployment are throwing a shadow over the continent's future. These trends are particularly worrying because individual alienation and fear of diversity are undermining political and economic development, breaking the links between generations and the network of social relations and associations that constitute the foundations of European society.

A NEW EUROPE

Paradoxically this ambivalence arises because we solved the greatest problems of the Old Continent in the twentieth century. These arose from the risk of large collective conflicts, either between states or between classes within a particular society. By integrating peoples, setting up legal frameworks for peaceful coexistence at international level and developing a social market economy, we were able to resolve and overcome most of these conflicts, even though clear inequalities remain (and are perhaps becoming more acute).

The new world that emerged after 1989 has brought new problems and has exacerbated old ones that have more to do with individuals than organized groups – problems such as identity in relation to other cultures, personal and environmental integrity in relation to technology, and the dignity of those who cannot manage to find a place in modern society.

In some ways, politics seem powerless to help in the face of these new problems that are shared by all European countries. Citizens accuse politicians of having lost contact with society and of taking decisions affecting the common good on the basis of oligarchical and inefficient practices. This poses the risk of the gradual alienation of individuals from their institutions and the generation of radicalism or apathy.

There are two distinct reasons for this professed powerlessness. First, new problems require new solutions, which are currently only at their research or experimental stage. After all, it has taken nearly a hundred years to overcome the problems created by nationalism and social conflict at the beginning of the twentieth century. Second, the majority of politically active organizations in Europe were born from the divisions that have marked this century. Now such divisions are much less pronounced, and those organizations are thus less able to tackle problems of a different nature.

Nearly all the contemporary political groupings are products of the great twentieth-century 'religious' conflicts between secularists and Catholics, socialists and liberals, and democrats and supporters of authoritarian regimes. They are therefore unsuited to meeting the great challenges of the twenty-first century, given that their ideological appeal and formulas for society are becoming obsolete.

This is why the challenges of modernity and modernization require *different political players* who are less tied to rigid ideologies and better able to bring together individuals and associations interested in the public good. Such organizations should be more open to civil society and to citizens, less obsessed with partisanship, and more interested in bringing together differing views at all levels of a government project. Parties are an essential element of democracy, because they allow citizens to participate in political life, choose their representatives in a transparent manner and mobilize consensus. But the 'quasi-religious' sectarian parties of the past can no longer meet the needs of European society and we therefore have to devise new forms of association that can provide practical answers to new and completely different problems. The manifestos of traditional parties are based on anachronistic questions like the class struggle or the cold war. Their leaderships reflect the personal consensus of their memberships, and justify their existence in terms of their own party lists rather than the good of their coalition or country. Any attempt to transform such parties or to reverse the transitional process that started a few years ago in Italy and elsewhere would be like trying to turn the clock back. It would be doomed to failure, because citizens are becoming increasingly detached, and traditional parties are unable to bring their priorities into line with the general interest rather than that of their own particular political group. What is more, completely outdated reflex actions still emerge in response to specific national and international questions, often of great importance.

The two most urgent questions, to which European politics must find innovative and effective answers, are how to reform the *European economic and social model* and how to deal with the anxieties relating to individual identity. In response to the first question, we need to fuse together the welfare state's collectivist tradition, which was the twentieth century's greatest achievement, and the ability to compete in a globalized economy, which is the twenty-first century's greatest challenge.

A rigid application of non-European models to the Old Continent's market would not only be questionable from a cultural point of view, but would force European firms to compete on an unfamiliar terrain with companies much better suited to these other models. Clearly, we must not abandon the social market economy. The task is to reform it and make it sustainable in the new international climate. In practice, this means limiting state intervention in order to prevent it stifling private enterprise and target it where it is most needed, in accordance with the principle of subsidiarity.

It is only by organizing a 'lean state' that European nations can now govern themselves. A 'lean state' is no less significant than a more cumbersome state apparatus, given that it can be more effective in carrying out its most important functions, while also strengthening relations with its own citizens. The 'lean state' does this first by concentrating its welfare activities on policies that promote human resources, health and education, and second by directing resources towards real needs, both old and new, rather than taking indiscriminate measures aimed at all citizens. We must also stimulate private enterprise directly, by promoting research and development particularly in the new electronic and communications technologies and in the increasingly strategic service sector. This means creating a capital market better suited to helping new businesses get started through mature financial markets and venture capital. Finally there must be a legal framework and a labour market that promote new initiatives.

New ethical challenges will become increasingly important, and it will be necessary to co-ordinate the relevant legislation at European level, to avoid destructive competition between the regulatory systems in different countries. The entire continent is affected by these 'life-and-death' issues, so policies on everything from immigration to bioethics will have to be more closely harmonized and perhaps put on a new basis.

The other great long-term political issue is of a cultural nature and creates the need for a common *education policy*. Educating and training the workforce provides the biggest contribution to growth in output over the long term. Moreover, ethical questions themselves ultimately depend on the cultural baggage that individuals carry around. Culture and education are the primary instruments for unifying the continent. The real challenge is to bring together in an unprecedented melting-pot not only the great Latin and Germanic cultures that produced the first European Community, but also the Anglo-Saxon culture, which joined later, and the Slav culture, which will soon be bursting onto the European scene.

All this means we will have to think in a new way about the educational question, and the link between education and the world of work. How can we produce highly educated Europeans who, in spite of their different roots, know how to engage in the kind of thorough and in-depth debate that is currently completely lacking? A 'European' ruling class could not be established without world-class educational centres of excellence that are truly international and multicultural.

One of the clearest and most alarming developments of the last generation is that the place for training the world's elite has increasingly shifted from the European universities to the American ones. Immediately after the war, by far the largest number of Asian, African and Latin-American leaders received their education at European universities, but now the great majority go to America. It will be difficult, if not impossible, to mould a common European spirit if we do not carry out this profound and impassioned 'cultural revolution', and do not meet the American challenge on the new horizons of science and technology.

The search for the European 'soul' increasingly appears to be the main issue affecting the future of our continent. We plan the way forward for European institutions (greater powers for the Parliament, restriction of the right of veto to exceptional cases and reorganization of the Commission and its powers), yet no one has any idea how to recreate the soul of Europe. This is indeed a sign of weakness. There is no dominant culture (I believe this to be our good fortune), and there are no philosophers, thinkers or 'opinion-makers' to whom we can refer at a continental level (which I regard as less positive). There is therefore the risk that European culture and values will go the way of the European financial markets. The euro is creating a single market out of many different forces, but the main actors in this unifying process are merchant banks and American investment funds. American culture in the wider sense of the term, symbolized by the mass media, is thought by some to be the only force capable of helping Europe find its own soul. There is nothing improper about such a suggestion, because, apart from anything else, the future equilibrium of the world rests on increasingly close political, economic and military co-operation between Europe and the United States, and this presupposes a degree of affinity over the fundamental models used to interpret our societies. However, I believe Europe has an enormous heritage that it can draw on, a heritage that must not be wasted because it is still the greatest wealth of culture and knowledge amassed by humanity.

Unfortunately there is no past experience and there are no set formulas that we can use to achieve this objective. The only thing we can do is to leave our current confusion behind us and seek out ways to overcome the dissipation of knowledge and culture. We need to defeat the Babel of languages by searching for a common understanding. We need a more genuine dialogue on how to build our common future. We cannot just stick with the past, and we cannot be happy with the formulas developed in the last century. European integration presents us with the ideal opportunity to re-examine this past, and compare it with the experiences of other peoples. It is our chance finally to free ourselves from legacies that were supposed to unite us but instead divided us.

Governments and peoples are not capable of breaking with the past and building a new future by themselves: this can only be done by all the peoples and governments of Europe working together. This is why Europe is so necessary: we cannot find the way forward on our own. As individual nations, we cannot even tackle the most elementary of our current problems, the greatest of which is our relationship with the people who surround us and look to us for their political and economic future. Germany, France and Italy are quite incapable of dealing with these problems on their own: only Europe can do that.

THE EUROPEAN UNION AFTER THE EURO

1999 was the year in which the euro was introduced. This was an essential milestone on the road to European integration, which has been resolutely supported by EU countries, though not without sacrifices. The euro has in fact unified a vast economic area with a gross domestic product comparable to America's. It is by far the strongest trading area in the world, and this provides European business with a horizon sufficiently vast to enable it to compete in a global economy. The euro has also made possible a massive operation to create economic stability, allowing it high growth without the danger of inflation. As occurred with the completion of the Common Market and the creation of the Single Market, it is now necessary to re-balance the political and institutional framework of the European edifice.

As far as economic policy is concerned, relinquishing monetary sovereignty has given added significance to taxation policies, which will have to be more closely co-ordinated so that they can play an effective stabilizing role when difficult events and situations develop in different countries and so that, over the long term, we can achieve genuine harmonization between the national economic systems. A further reason for co-ordinating our economic policies is that regional economies will diverge in the initial period after monetary union. The wealthier regions will be better able to exploit the new opportunities over the short term, thus increasing their national earnings. The risk therefore is that the more backward regions will be left behind. This problem will have to be dealt with through budget reform.

The Union's citizens have more than merely economic aspirations: they are looking for a more effective integration of other aspects of their lives. It is therefore possible to foresee, early in the twenty-first century, a rapid completion of the process that will lead to the creation of a genuine European citizenship. This will establish minimum social and political rights along the lines of the European Charter and the Social Chapter. Perhaps we should have the courage to start the new millennium with the decision to make all citizens born in countries within the Union citizens of Europe as well. The rules governing EU citizenship could act as a focal point for national reforms in dismantling the 'heavy state', for instance strengthening the civil and commercial law to the detriment of the state's 'administrative' role in the nineteenth-century sense.

The Union also has an increasing responsibility in the world, due to its position, its tradition of safeguarding peace and human rights, and its interest in having a stable international environment in which to achieve its own commercial ambitions. For this purpose, the EU, in conjunction with the WEU and an appropriate 'fourth pillar', must develop the capacity to defend itself by rationalizing the use of industrial resources and military infrastructures, so that it can actively help maintain regional stability and fight against major international dangers, the greatest of which is the proliferation of weapons of mass destruction.

While tying economic prosperity and trade to political stability, the EU must continue along the road of multilateral liberalization within the World Trade Organization to prevent a damaging return to protectionism at national or continental level, and to give developing regions access to developed markets, which is the best way to help them grow. The consequence of growth in markets is that there must be proper protection of the environment, in order to achieve really *sustainable* growth. Europe must complete the process of bringing the candidate countries into an enlarged EU, so as to heal once and for all the continent's divisions without losing its internal cohesion. Finally, Europe must pursue a policy of partnership and co-operation with the former Soviet Union and, above all, the Mediterranean region, in order to create a vast area of stability with a free market, in which the EU can prosper and invest.

The Mediterranean must be the other face of Europe. There must be greater awareness of Mediterranean issues and more innovative proposals put forward by Italy, France and Spain. This is certainly not an attempt to counterbalance enlargement, but simply to allow the creation of an area of peace and development along Europe's most difficult and unpredictable border. Our relationship with the Islamic world will decide the quality of our future. It is a question that requires intelligence, the ability to put forward political solutions and great faith in the prospects of peaceful coexistence between peoples. For Italy there is an added bonus: it is a precondition for the development and prosperity of the Mezzogiorno. However, I do not believe that any single country can impose this relationship by itself. Either it is a relationship involving Europe as a whole or it will be incapable of creating any hope of change.

Such ambitious tasks cannot be pursued for long with the current Community institutions, which the Treaty of Amsterdam has only started to reform. Besides, enlargement itself requires change, as institutions designed for six member states cannot meet the needs of twenty or twenty-five member states. Useful proposals have already been tabled for reforming the Commission's composition, and these could adapt the decision-making processes to the new situation. However, the democratic legitimacy of the increasingly important European institutions and the efficacy of the Union's policies demand a more ambitious project giving greater powers to the Parliament in joint decision-making, increasing the use of majority voting in the Council and introducing an electoral procedure for choosing the president of the Commission.

Italy in Europe

In this new and more ambitious Europe that can meet the needs of its citizens as well as those of its governments, Italy too must become more European, in order to make a better contribution to the Union's aims and to be more adept at putting its own point of view across. For this reason, it is essential to complete the transformation of Italy's political system, as can be seen from the essential role played by stable government over the years in which convergence with the Maastricht criteria was required.

Economic stability

In mid-1996, Italy was still outside all five of the Maastricht parameters (the budget deficit and inflation were still too high, there was too great a difference between Italian and German interest rates, and, what is more, the lira was outside the EMS). Italy, one of the Community's founding members, was in considerable danger of being left outside the great adventure of the single currency. It is true that for some years, since 1992–3 in fact, Italy had set itself on the road to recovery by finally asserting a 'culture of stability' within its borders. In spite of this, the rate of Italy's convergence with the Union's healthier economies, although consistent, would have failed to comply with the schedule for monetary union.[1]

Many reflections could be made on this journey towards recovery, and many facts related to it. We will be looking into some of these in the following pages. At this point, I would like to recall what should be considered a turning-point in any

cool-headed historical reappraisal: that is my letter as prime
minister of Italy to President Chirac and Chancellor Kohl of
6 September 1996. On 31 August of that year, the traditional
Franco-German Summit had been held, and it reiterated the
objective of commencing EMU [translator's note: Economic
and Monetary Union] from 1 January 1999. A few days later,
I wrote the same letter to both leaders:

> In view of the lively debate in Europe on this subject [EMU],
> you have rightly decided to demonstrate that the time-scale
> for achieving EMU will be strictly adhered to, as it constitutes
> an absolute priority for the Union and for countries that firmly
> believe in this project. Its failure would deal a very serious
> blow to the entire process of European integration. Italy is fun-
> damentally committed to achieving this objective and we will
> pursue that commitment with the utmost determination.

Thus, when it came to the budget for 1997, the Italian government decided to accelerate recovery by concentrating its
efforts on reducing the budget deficit – the most sensitive
of the Maastricht parameters – to less than 3 per cent in 1997.[2]
The lira's re-entry into the EMS exchange-rate mechanism at
the end of November 1996, after four whole years outside it,
was an essential step towards the future single currency and
the first great success resulting from the efforts of previous
years.

Political stability

Strengthening the first-past-the-post element in electoral law
is not enough on its own to achieve political stability. You also
have to deal with the party system if you want to switch to a
bipartisan system that really works, which is the best guarantee
of stable government and the best chance to provide the electors
with a choice between coherent and modern programmes. We
also need to be able to supplement these reforms with the
appropriate institutional reforms.

   Another point is that we must pursue our attempts to achieve
a 'lean state'. This is partly an economic question, as it requires

strengthening the state's role as arbiter rather than as a direct producer of goods and services, and it is partly a reform of the civil service, which Italians perceive as the country's least 'European' element. For this purpose, the principle of subsidiarity both in relation to the market and to local governmental bodies, in accordance with the logic of decentralization, is the key to better integration of Italy's society and economy into Europe, carrying on along the road to recovery required by the stability pact.

These are just a few of the things that Europe, and in particular Italy, needs to do in the next few years. Although they are avowedly ambitious, these are necessary reforms which, like all the past sacrifices in the name of integration, will lead to even greater rewards. We only have to remember Europe's role in consolidating Italy's democracy, and later in spreading a more rigorous economic policy and a more modern form of capitalism. For Italy, Europe has always represented an example of rectitude. This is why the enlargement of the European Union and the promotion of its values over an even larger area are the greatest contributions we can make to political and economic development. This is why future European governments must follow in the footsteps of their far-sighted founding fathers, so that they can offer generations to come a secure and prosperous future.

ACKNOWLEDGEMENTS

I would like to thank all the friends who have enabled this book to be written by engaging in the intellectual debate that evolved throughout my years as prime minister and, in many cases, continues to this day. Among the many people to whom I am indebted, I would particularly like to mention Paolo Onofri, Giulio Santagata, Gianfranco Brunelli, Filippo Andreatta, Bruno Manghi, Franco Pizzetti, Armando Varricchio and Stefano Jedrkiewica. This book could not have been written without them. However, my special thanks go to Franco Mosconi, because, as well as his involvement in the intellectual debate, he also did an exceptional job on checking the economic data and the stages in the process of institutional integration. I also wish to thank David Crowther, David Monkcom and David Skinner for their valuable work in revising the manuscript. Finally, I could

not forget Ambassador Roberto Nigido who has accompanied me
every day on the actual and the intellectual journey towards European unity.

This volume includes lectures and public discussion papers given
in various international forums. The first three chapters contain
reflections expressed at the London School of Economics and Political Science on the occasion of the LSE Founders' Day Lecture for
the 1997–8 academic year (London, 26 January 1998), my address
to the French National Assembly (Paris, 19 November 1997) and
the lecture I gave at the Grandes Conférences Catholiques (Brussels,
18 November 1997). Chapter 4 develops arguments that I examined
on two separate occasions in the United States: my speech to the
Chicago Council on Foreign Relations at the end of an official visit
to the United States (Washington and Chicago, 5–8 May 1998) and
the lecture I gave at the Paul H. Nitze School of Advanced International Studies, part of the Johns Hopkins University (Washington,
DC, 24 November 1998). The chapters in part II use material from
my inaugural lecture to the Real Academia de Ciencias Morales y
Políticas when I became an honorary member (Madrid, 25 November 1997), and the lecture I gave at the Universitat Politécnica de
Catalunya on receiving an honorary degree (Barcelona, 3 December
1998). The chapters in part III draw on the lecture I gave on receiving an honorary degree in economics at Madras University (Chennai,
India, 8 January 1998), reflections on the future of European industry
and finance I expressed at the twentieth Jean Monnet Conference,
held at the European University Institute (Fiesole, Florence, 20 March
1998), the lecture given at the Real Academia de Ciencias Morales y
Políticas (Madrid, 3 December 1998), and my opening speech to the
1998 meeting of the Frankfurt European Banking Congress (Frankfurt, 20 November 1998).

Notes

1   In December 1995, the Madrid European Council decided to
    send a strong signal of commitment to European integration. The
    heads of state and government confirmed the recommendations
    issued by the finance ministers in September of that year. Thus they
    put a strict interpretation on the Maastricht Treaty, which left open
    the question of the reference year for the 'photograph' of the
    economic and financial situations of member states. Rather than
    using the data for the 1998 *forecasts*, it was determined in Madrid
    that the decision on which countries would be allowed to take
    part in monetary union had to be based on the *final data* for 1997.

2   It should be noted that at the time of the Madrid European Council (see previous note), the Italian Parliament had already approved the Finance Act and the budget for 1996, which provided for a programme of convergence in relation to the Maastricht Treaty, to be completed in 1998. The new situation created by the Madrid Summit and the Franco-German 'push' therefore made it necessary during 1996 to adopt severe measures to bring the European target forward by a year. The previous 1997 budget adjustment of 32,500 billion lire was increased by 37,000 billion. In addition, the government proposed and the Parliament approved a 'tax for Europe' totalling 25,000 billion lire. The entire package of 62,500 billion lire was aimed at reducing the budget deficit, in relation to the gross domestic product, to the 3% level by the end of 1997. This was the largest financial adjustment ever approved in the absence of a crisis on the currency markets. When the final data was released, the reduction proved to be even greater, bringing the deficit down to 2.7%, as demonstrated by the convergence reports for the European Commission issued by the European Monetary Institute.

Part I

United Europe: Half a Century in the Making

1

A vision of Europe

Europe means many things at the dawn of the twenty-first century. It means a large single market and a stimulating competitive environment, both capable of generating prosperity and technological innovation. It means a social model founded on individual rights, which has given rise to a degree of social cohesion that hasn't been equalled anywhere else in the world. It means a great power that can play a significant role on the world stage. And yet, in recent years, Europe has meant, more than anything else, the challenge of the single currency. This is the argument to which I will initially devote my attention, and I will return to the other points in due course.

(1) Economic and Monetary Union (EMU) represents, with the creation of the euro, an act of faith in Europe and, at the same time, a challenge in the wider context of the global economy. It is an unprecedented historical event.[1] All things considered, the renunciation of one's right to coin money is a huge *political* decision. The state is, in fact, giving up one of its most cherished instruments of sovereignty. At the threshold of the twenty-first century, this instrument is more visible than military sovereignty itself, symbolized by the sword.

But the euro also poses a challenge to the world economy of our times. With a single currency, the EMU member states will be better able to confront recurrent upheavals on the financial markets. What is more, the single currency is the crowning achievement of the 'single market' that we have been building. Indeed, only with a single currency can true freedom of movement of all production factors (goods, people, services and capital) come fully into effect. In short, only a single currency will allow us to have a truly common market.

Recent world events give us reason to look to the future with a degree of optimism. During the period of the 'Asian crisis', the European currencies fluctuated together, as a *group* of currencies, while in similar situations in the not too distant past, it was the German mark that gained in value against the majority of the currencies in the EMS.[2] Such synchronized currency fluctuations in the run-up to EMU is further confirmation that the path we took several years ago was the right one.[3] It is objective proof that the monetary system, which we Europeans have been establishing at supranational level, works and works well.

(2) Having just completed the 'convergence' years dictated by the Maastricht Treaty,[4] which produced better results than expected, we now find ourselves on the verge of important changes to the *collective structures* that govern the workings of economic and social life in European countries. We are facing permanent transformations rather than temporary modifications.

At least since the first oil crisis in the early seventies, Western countries have been living through a kind of 'age of uncertainty'. The uncertainty was and still is related to the redistribution of the world's resources. However, you have to think of the new players who have entered the global economy and are continuing to do so. Today, redistribution is no longer achieved by increasing the prices of raw materials (which generates inflation), but rather by the efforts of emerging countries to increase their market share of manufacturing production. In the seventies, many countries – including Italy – failed to perceive the need to review collective behaviour and individual expectations: today there is a new awareness.

Moreover, the production process now appears to have a completely new and inherent feature that could profoundly affect the social fabric. Whereas the old-fashioned 'Fordist' mass production tended to generate greater equality in the distribution of income, today's new systems of production based on electronics and information technology tend to generate inequality. In other words, they are widening the gap between the 'literate' and the 'illiterate', the included and the excluded, the insider and the outsider. On this point, Peter Glotz's theory of the society of 'two-thirds', which was taken up in a different way by Ralf Dahrendorf, is very instructive. Until a few years ago, the distinction was between the two-thirds of the citizens who were in secure positions and the remaining third who were marginalized from the economic process and driven outside the political process. In the current situation, however, the distinction is between the percentage of citizens who are in possession of new forms of expertise and the percentage of those who are not.

(3) All the economic and social changes that I have briefly described have resulted in an enormous increase in the number of people who are obliged to survive by relying on benefits from the welfare system: in others words, the excluded. This means that there is an essential realignment to which welfare systems must adapt, and this realignment is of a *macroeconomic* nature. Given scant budget resources or, to be more precise, a situation where states are facing a taxation crisis, cutting welfare benefits is the only way to reallocate limited resources to those who are suffering the greatest economic and social hardship.

In reality, there is a second and no less important realignment that has to be sought when Western societies get down to refashioning their welfare systems: these systems will have to adjust to new forms of employment, new jobs and the new model of social mobility. The European response to the challenge of Asian capitalism cannot be to abandon the 'European model' of social cohesion, but rather to reform it, hopefully in a systematic manner.

Over the years, the various welfare systems have been important instruments for eliminating class differences, thus developing a mechanism for social integration and promoting national identity. The success of these systems coincided – and this was no accident – with the most vigorous period of economic growth Europe has known. Today, the return to a satisfactory rate of economic growth appears once again to be closely related to our ability to steer a course through domestic and international competition. The overall efficiency of any economic system can be reduced by welfare systems that create distortions in incentives. There is an inherent need to restrain the growth of welfare expenditure in all European countries to deal with the ageing population and increasing international competition. This need is made all the greater by the requirement to achieve full macroeconomic convergence and comply with the Stability and Growth Pact.[5] Yet, we might wonder whether these cuts in expenditure could impede the shift towards a new European national identity? And if this were the case, what kind of Europe would we be creating for ourselves and the coming generations once this process has been completed?

(4) Welfare systems, by their very nature, find themselves at the junction between all these problems. The welfare state that Italy created was, moreover, characterized by its own particular anomalies. Above all, it provided overprotection for certain social groups and types of risk, and inadequate protection of other groups and risks. An excessive proportion of its resources were distributed through the pension system.[6] This is why the reform of the welfare state has been for several months at the top of Italy's political agenda.

The Convergence Programme, submitted by the Italian government, approved by the Ecofin Committee in January 1998,[7] and then approved by Parliament at the end of 1997 together with the 1998 Finance Act, outlined a reasonable and achievable path to the new welfare state based on 'opportunities'. The interaction between the forces of the free market and competition on the one hand and equality of opportunity for all citizens on the other is the 'master plan' for building the new Europe.

(5) As the 1980s gave way to the 1990s, political and economic debate in many places was centred upon the distinction between the two principal 'models of capitalism', the Anglo-Saxon one and the Germano-Japanese one (or, if you prefer, the 'Rhineland model'). At first sight, the essential difference between the two models appeared to be of a financial nature, concerning the prevailing methods of funding businesses. The

pivotal role played by stock exchanges in Anglo-Saxon countries therefore contrasted with the pre-eminence of the 'mixed bank' in Germany and other countries that followed its example. On closer inspection, however, the financial aspect did not fully explain all the differences, which in fact concerned other areas of economic and social life, such as the protection of citizens in times of need and the availability of jobs offered by the system.

For many years, the German model was widely considered to be superior from both an economic and a social point of view, as it was capable of producing the best combination of efficiency and equity, and of economic growth and social cohesion. Today, some years later, the rivalry between the two models continues. As often occurs in history, the pendulum has swung the other way. The United States can now boast an excellent economic and financial performance, an unchallenged technological leadership and, above all, the creation of millions of new jobs at a rate that shows no signs of slackening. Conversely, as we all know, unemployment in the European Union has reached levels that can no longer be tolerated socially.[8] Sustained economic growth, combined with a flexible labour market, is at the root of the American success.

In judging the economic and social profile of these so-called 'models of capitalism', an additional factor must be taken into account: the degree of inequality in the distribution of income. A high level of inequality is in fact damaging for growth, because it excludes too many potential players from economic life, and because it can lead to inappropriate economic policies. From this point of view, the countries of continental Europe, with their extensive welfare systems, have produced the best results. In these countries, the distribution of income is generally less unequal. Put simply, the distinction between the two models of capitalism can now be seen as a distinction between two different welfare systems. In fact, the financial institutions of the two models tend to become increasingly similar: in all economic systems, stock exchanges and banks are complementary mechanisms for the allocation of funds.

On the other hand, this is not the case with public welfare systems and programmes. The most demanding task facing Western societies at the dawn of the new century is that of combining equity and social cohesion (which are not only moral values but also economic factors) with the appropriate flexibility of the labour market (which means greater job opportunities for their citizens). The European model is always contrasted with the American one. And, as we have seen, the pendulum swings back and forth. Economic history offers us some useful lessons.

(6) I have always been firmly convinced that macroeconomic stability is a fundamental prerequisite for achieving prolonged and sustained economic growth. From this point of view, the drastic reduction in inflation by all member states of the European Union,[9] including Italy, can be seen as a great triumph and a necessary step in the fight against unemployment. The most tangible result of macroeconomic stability is the decline in interest rates,[10] to the benefit of corporate and family investments.

An essential part of any serious policy for economic stabilization is reducing the deficit and public borrowing. This is particularly true in many of our European countries, where public debt has reached levels no longer compatible with sustainable economic growth.[11] Good financial management and meeting the Maastricht criteria represent two interconnected results, both directed at imposing a limit – a just and appropriate limit – on government action. They cannot leave a mountain of debts to be inherited by later generations. The Maastricht Treaty imposed good financial management, but this is a valid target in itself, precisely because it contributes to equity between generations.

(7) All member states of the European Union felt closely involved in the task of creating monetary union, irrespective of whether they had decided to be members right from the start on 1 January 1999. However, as I pointed out at the beginning, monetary union is only a part of the wider prospect of European integration. I personally took part in the negotiations between heads of state and government that led to important breakthroughs on the long road to integration. I am thinking particularly of the European Summit in Amsterdam (16–17 June 1997), in which we reached political agreement

on the new treaty and the green light was given to enlargement of the European Union, and of the Extraordinary Summit on Employment held in Luxembourg on 20–1 of November of the same year.

I am convinced that it is only at supranational (that is, European) level that our individual countries can meet the great challenges they are facing. But to reach this objective we need to strengthen our common institutions, and adapt them to enlargement and a constantly changing international context. We are formulating a genuinely European foreign policy and a joint policy on immigration and asylum rights, and we are setting up a common social framework within which to achieve effective economic union.

The Treaty of Amsterdam

The European Summit that concluded the six months of the Dutch presidency took important decisions in pursuit of these goals. It was particularly encouraging that the Social Chapter was inserted in the treaty. The British government adopted a constructive approach, thus contributing to this significant result. Moreover, the Common Foreign and Security Policy (CFSP) was strengthened, although not to the extent one might have hoped.

Enlargement to the East

I have just mentioned the enormous step taken towards enlargement to embrace new member states. A Europe that is expanding is a dynamic Europe which, as stated in the founding Treaty of Rome,[12] is open to all European countries that share its values and intend to pursue its common policies. For the first time in its history, enlargement will take our Community beyond that line which, until a few years ago, we were in the habit of calling the Iron Curtain. The significance, partly symbolic, of this transition is something we should take pride in, and at the same time, it should encourage us to make further progress.[13]

An enlarged European Union must be equipped with institutional structures capable of making it work. In practice, this means taking up the debate on reforms precisely where it was left off on the last night of the Amsterdam European Council – in particular with regard to the questions of weighting votes in the Council of Ministers, a significant extension of majority voting and a reduction in the number of commissioners. If these changes are not fully implemented, it will not be possible to ensure that the Union functions properly and that we achieve the ambitious goals we have set ourselves. This is why Italy, France and Belgium have jointly stated that we must further reform the European institutions *before* enlargement takes place.

The Summit on Employment

The heads of state and government who met in Luxembourg for the Special Summit agreed upon the need to strengthen the social dimension of European economic policies. The principal responsibility for employment policy remains with the individual member states. It is mainly up to them to provide market players with an economic environment favourable to the creation of new jobs. However, when unemployment reaches today's levels and proves to be apparently impervious to measures taken in individual sectors, it becomes increasingly clear that a solution has to be found at a supranational level. Being fully aware of this, Tony Blair, Goran Persson and I signed and presented a joint declaration on the eve of the Luxembourg Summit. We argued that in order to create new jobs we must improve the competitiveness of companies and the employability of our workforces, and strengthen the single market by removing barriers to the free movement of all production factors (capital, labour, goods and services). We must pay greater attention to small and medium-sized enterprises, and constantly maintain training standards for our workforce.

The European Union could make a significant contribution by regulating incentives and directing more Community funds into job-creation schemes. If Europe as a whole cannot provide genuine answers to the legitimate demand for employment coming from its (many) unemployed citizens, it will run the risk of losing the consensus on which our adventure is founded.

(8) Thus we find ourselves faced with the task of making the European Union's institutions more effective, enlarging the Community to embrace new members and creating new employment. All three objectives go beyond the abilities of our individual nations. They are objectives that complement the blueprint for the single currency by helping to make the new Europe more efficient and competitive. But we have to be clear on this point. In order to compete on the new global stage with reasonable chances of success, Europe must again seize the leadership role that for centuries was its boast: leadership in production and technology, and intellectual and cultural leadership. We have to close the gap that has opened up in recent years as a result of the transfer of the most modern centres of research and development (R&D) from Europe to other parts of the world, as these are pivotal to modern methods of production. We have to realize that the vast resources and equipment required by research activity imply extremely large enterprises that benefit from the economies of scale.

We need to concentrate our efforts on methods by which we could exploit in the best possible manner the immense heritage of expertise and culture that makes what we call Europe distinctive. I am particularly concerned that we bring our best researchers and scholars, who today are scattered around the world, back to our European schools and universities. The young people who came from the whole of the then known world to the universities of medieval Europe accumulated and spread the knowledge of the past and laid the foundations of modern science. The challenge that now faces us is to transform this heritage into new opportunities for growth and employment. Our commitment to the future can only find expression in the context of Europe.

(9) To summarize, EMU will alter the balance of the international monetary system. The creation of the euro will lead to revolutionary changes once it emerges as the new 'reserve currency' on a par with the dollar. This, in turn, will give rise to a more complex and at the same time more stable international

monetary system no longer based on just one currency. Indeed, the international financial order will no longer be influenced solely by events occurring within one particular economy. Quite the contrary, it will be able to rely upon a wider range of strong currencies, and this will limit the risks of turbulence in the currency markets. I therefore believe that the euro will create opportunities and will have a positive impact on the world economy, although it will require careful consultation and diplomacy. Europe will accept greater responsibility in the monetary field as it already has in international trade.

Enlargement to include the countries of central and eastern Europe will increase the Union's territory in quantitative terms by about 30 per cent, while its population and gross domestic product will increase by 29 and 10 per cent respectively. Having these countries as members will profoundly change Europe's political framework as we have known it for the last fifty years and will, in a sense, put the final seal on the process of reunifying the two halves of Europe that started when the Iron Curtain collapsed in 1989.

The ultimate result of enlargement will be a greater, more self-confident Europe with a greater interest in maintaining stable international relations. The Union's strategic profile will also be enhanced as it builds closer relations with the other geopolitical regions to the east and south-east. Europe will therefore take greater responsibilities upon itself and will have to develop a genuinely global outlook. This is particularly true of its relations with the two great regions of the Middle East, where our most important security interests lie, and South-East Asia, which is rapidly becoming one of our major trading partners.

None of this in any way supports the theory, so dear to Samuel Huntington, of a growing 'clash of civilizations',[14] and the consequent need to prepare for a conflict between different cultures. Relations within these regions are very complex and call for attention and skilful diplomacy, rather than schematic generalizations. We must resist the temptation to erect a 'Fortress Europe' dividing us from the rest of the world: this would be short-sighted and lead to instability. We must therefore act as reliable mediators in regional conflicts, expand our economic diplomacy to develop relations with such important regions and take the opportunity to improve the social systems of strategic countries like China and Iran by bringing them into the great family of nations.

With the memory of its bitter rivalries in the past, Europe today is aware that its primary interest lies in helping to develop a strong and prosperous global economy rather than pursuing some form of national ascendancy. Strengthened by this knowledge, we must help other countries to understand that isolation and dogmatic attitudes are counter-productive, and that the real interests of great nations are political and economic development, rather than hegemony. Regional players are often too engrossed in questions relating to some particular historical contingency to be able to realize this elementary truth. It is in this light that the role of a major external mediator can be essential. This is why I am so persuaded that Europe will play an increasingly important role on the international stage, even though the common foreign and defence policy has not yet taken shape.

(10) The future of Europe is important not only for its own citizens and enterprises, but also for the wider international community. The Europe established by the Treaty of Rome has come to represent a genuine model of integration for other countries to follow. The productive and peaceful settlement of ancient conflicts (such as those between France and Germany and between Romania and Hungary) has given hope that other regional conflicts could be solved. Europe's founding fathers were aiming at peace after centuries of war. After several decades, the pacification of the Old Continent, which was the heart of their grand design, has now been fully realized. Today, we have entered a new era in which Europe is taking on greater responsibilities directed at managing international relations.

I stated several years ago that 'Europe is one of the great success stories of our time'.[15] I said it in spite of all the uncertainties that surrounded Europe at that time. I believe in all sincerity that this vision has been borne out by the events of these last months, which have seen the achievement of EMU's 'convergence' criteria and the beginning of the EU's enlargement to the east. In spite of many difficulties and obstacles, we are building a greater and more integrated Europe, which will be a key player in the new international politics.

Notes

1 There have certainly been other examples of monetary union. In particular, there was the Latin Union which was established in 1865 between France, Belgium, Switzerland, Italy, the Papal State and, at a later stage, Greece and Romania. In this union each country maintained its own currency which was convertible into precious metals (gold and silver). Then there was the monetary union established in 1921 between Belgium and Luxembourg in which the currencies of the two countries coexisted (the Belgian franc and the Luxembourg franc). 'Our' monetary union represents something unique, if we consider both the actual strength of the eleven countries taking part (Austria, Belgium, Finland, France, Germany, Ireland, Italy, Luxembourg, Holland, Portugal and Spain, while Great Britain, Denmark, Greece and Sweden are for the moment outside) and the institutional framework that supports it. Suffice it to say that: (i) the eleven members are adopting a single currency, the euro, which will replace their respective national currencies; (ii) monetary policy has been transferred to a supranational level and put in the hands of the European Central Bank, which is an institution independent of the governments; (iii) the budgetary policies of the participating countries comply with the restrictions on public borrowing imposed by the Stability and Growth Pact (see n. 5).

2 The European Monetary System (EMS), created by the French president Valéry Giscard d'Estaing and the German chancellor Helmut Schmidt, constituted an important stage in the creation of a stable currency area for Europe. Introduced in March 1979, it was from an operational point of view a system of 'fixed' but 'adjustable' exchange rates, in the sense that for every pair of currencies it determined a 'central parity' and 'margins of fluctuation' around this parity.

3 European currencies fluctuated in the months between the 'Asian crisis' (which began in May 1997 when the Thai baht became the object of speculation) and the formal decision on each country's admission to EMU, taken by the European Summit in Brussels (the Community body that convenes the heads of state and heads of government) on 2–3 May 1998. This decision was largely expected following the two Convergence Reports drawn up by the European Commission and the European Monetary Institute and made public on 25 March 1998.

4 The provisions of the Maastricht Treaty known as the 'five convergence criteria' (articles 104c and 109j, as specified in Protocol

no. 6 on convergence criteria appended to the treaty): (i) *price stability* (i.e. an inflation rate not exceeding the average for the three countries with the lowest inflation by more than 1.5 percentage points); (ii) *long-term interest rates* (which must not exceed by more than 2 percentage points that of the three member states which have achieved the best results in terms of price stability); (iii) and (iv) sustainability of the public finances which, in turn, means the ratio between the *public deficit* and the gross domestic product (GDP) not exceeding 3%, and the ratio between *public debt* and GDP not exceeding 60%, 'unless the ratio is falling at a sufficient degree and is approaching the reference value at an adequate rate' (see art. 104c); (v) *exchange-rate stability* (i.e. compliance with the normal margins of fluctuation provided in the EMS exchange-rate mechanism for at least two years without devaluation against the currency of any other member state).

5 Adopted at the European Summit in Dublin (December 1996, amended at the Amsterdam Summit of 1997), the Stability and Growth Pact fixed the rules for conducting fiscal policy immediately after the launch of the euro. The starting-point was the main Maastricht criteria, i.e. a budget deficit not exceeding 3% of GDP, unless there are 'exceptional circumstances' that justify breaking through the ceiling. The pact automatically recognizes exceptional circumstances when the GDP falls by 2% or more, or when the fall in output is between 0.75 and 2%. The Ecofin Committee decides by a qualified majority on whether exceptional circumstances exist or not. If, in the absence of exceptional circumstance an excessive deficit is not corrected by appropriate measures, the member-state will be called upon to deposit with the European Union a sum without interest equal to 0.2% of the GDP plus one-tenth of the excess deficit above 3%, up to a maximum of 0.5% of the GDP. Finally, if the deficit stays above the limit for two years, the deposit is forfeited. As has been pointed out, there was also a decision on the pact at the Amsterdam Summit. In this resolution, the members 'undertake to comply with the medium-term objective of a balanced budget or a budget surplus in their stability and convergence programmes'. It later states that: 'Compliance with this objective will allow member-states to manage the normal cyclical fluctuations while maintaining a deficit within the reference value of 3% of GDP' (cf. EU Commission, *European Economy*, 64 (Brussels: 1997)).

6 The *Final Report* of the Commission examining the macroeconomic compatibility of welfare spending set up by the Prime Minister's Office and chaired by Paolo Onofri, states that:

from a comparative perspective, the situation in our country appears to reflect several clear anomalies. Italy spends about a quarter of its GDP on social services as a whole (as defined by Eurostat), an expenditure level not dissimilar to the average figure for the twelve countries in the European Union in 1994. Italy does not therefore appear to be 'out of line' in terms of being either above or below the aggregate figure. The great anomaly in the Italian situation concerns the way in which that expenditure breaks down. European comparisons reveal marked abnormalities: one abnormality concerns areas of *risk*, and another concerns the protected *categories*.

As far as the risks are concerned, the percentage of resources allocated to protecting 'old age and victims of accidents and natural disasters' seems to be significantly higher than in the other countries: 61.5% of total welfare expenditure, as against a Community average of 45.3%. Expenditure covering risks categorized as 'unemployment/training', 'family/maternity', 'accommodation' and 'other welfare' receives a very much lower proportion of welfare spending than elsewhere in Europe (18.4% compared with 31.9%). Our country is in line with the others on health expenditure, which is allocated the average funding for the twelve European countries of about one-sixth of welfare spending.

7   The Ecofin Committee (the Community body that convenes the treasury and finance ministers of the member states) recommended to Italy, as it did to the other member states, that it should present its own Convergence Programme (see Minister of Finance, Budget and Economic Planning, *Italian Convergence Programme 1997*, Rome: 1997). This was a programme that documented recent progress in attaining the Maastricht criteria and set a series of reform targets over the medium to long term. The Italian government presented its programme on 30 May 1997, based on the forecasts and findings of the Economic and Financial Planning Document (EFPD) for the years 1998–2000. The Ecofin Committee approved the programme in July of the same year. The third part of the Convergence Programme was entirely devoted to structural reforms, commencing with those concerning welfare.

8   At the end of 1998, the average unemployment rate both for the EU and the Euroland countries was about 11% and in some areas rose to 15–20%. On the other hand, the United States ended the same year with an unemployment rate of 4.3%. The question of possible policies to deal with unemployment will be dealt with in ch. 10.

9   A glance at the 'Essential characteristics of the euro zone', published in the *ECB Monthly Bulletin* (January 1999, p. 12), will confirm this: in November 1998 consumer price inflation in Euroland was 0.9%. When the EU countries approved and signed the Maastricht Treaty (1991–2), inflation was fluctuating between 5% and 4.5% (see OECD, *Economic Outlook*, various years).

10 We also learn from the *Bulletin* published by the European Central Bank in Frankfurt that the three-month interest rate in Euroland at the end of 1998 was 3.25%, while the yield on ten-year government securities (the long-term interest rate) was 3.94%. Here again, there is a big contrast with the period when the treaty was signed: the area that today constitutes Euroland had long-term interest rates in 1991–2 averaging about 10% (see OECD, *Economic Outlook*).

11 At the end of 1998, the budget deficit in Euroland (see European Central Bank *Bulletin*) as a percentage of GDP was 2.3%, while public debt as a percentage of GDP was 73.8%. At the time of the Maastricht Treaty, the deficit for the countries now in Euroland was between 4.5% and 5%, and public debt was about 65% (see OECD, *Economic Outlook*).

12 As is well known, the process of European integration took its first step with the establishment of the European Coal and Steel Community, which was signed on 18 April 1951. Then came the Treaty of Rome, signed in the Capitol on 25 March 1957, which established the European Economic Community (EEC). Although United Europe has been enriched by numerous other common institutions in the more than forty intervening years, the Treaty of Rome has maintained its special centrality. 'Although it wasn't the first brick to be laid', Tommaso Padoa-Schioppa has asserted, 'the Treaty of Rome constituted the decisive step towards an organic supranational power. From today's perspective, the Treaty was not (as even Jean Monnet and many other federalists thought) simply an international free-trade agreement: it was also the nucleus of the Constitution for the European Union. It was a *Treaty*, it is true, in the sense that it was written in the traditional format of a contractual text between governments, subject to ratification by the parliaments. But it was also a *Constitution*, in the sense that it transformed our entire economic and legal order and supplemented the constitutions of the member states' (T. Padoa-Schioppa, *Che cosa ci ha insegnato l'avventura europea*, Bologna: Il Mulino, 1998).

13   The enlargement of the Union has been at the top of the political agenda for some time. On 26 and 27 June 1995 the European Council of Cannes decided that negotiations on Cyprus's
membership would commence six months after the end of the
Intergovernmental Conference reviewing the treaties (another
Mediterranean country, Malta, had in the meantime decided to
withdraw its candidature). At the Madrid Summit in December
of the same year, the hope was expressed that membership
negotiations for all the associate countries in central and eastern
Europe could commence six months after the conclusion of
the Intergovernmental Conference. Furthermore, the European
Council instructed the Commission to prepare its judgements
on the applications submitted by each candidate country, as
required by the treaty. In June 1997, the Intergovernmental
Conference concluded its deliberations. The Amsterdam European Council therefore acknowledged that it was now possible
to proceed with enlargement. On 16 July, the Commission
submitted its judgements on the degree to which the ten candidate countries of central and eastern Europe were prepared
for membership. It considered the political and economic criteria
to have been satisfied in five countries: Estonia, Poland, the Czech
Republic, Slovenia and Hungary. In the case of Cyprus, the Commission restated the favourable judgement it had given back
in 1993. In December 1997, the Luxembourg European Council authorized the commencement of six Intergovernmental Conferences for the formal membership negotiations with Cyprus,
Estonia, Poland, the Czech Republic, Slovenia and Hungary.
On 12 March 1998, the first European conference of heads of
state and government from EU countries and applicant countries
met in London. A recent book throws light on the 'rules' which
could bring about beneficial coexistence in a future Europe enlarged to 800 million people: M. Emerson, *Redrawing the Map
of Europe* (New York: St Martin's Press, 1998).

14   S. Huntington, *The Clash of Civilizations and the Remaking of
World Order* (London: Touchstone, 1998).

15   I refer here to a lecture I gave at the London School of Economics
and Political Science in January 1996, during a visit to the
British capital to present to the political, financial and academic
community in Britain the political programme of the Ulivo
('Olive-Tree') coalition ahead of the 1996 Italian general elec-
tion [translator's note: the Ulivo coalition is the left-of-centre
electoral coalition formed around the former Communist Party,
now the Democratic Party of the Left].

2

Latin culture and Germanic culture in the creation of Europe

(1) Two neo-Latin nations, Italy and France, were at the forefront of moves towards European unification fifty years ago when the embryo of political and cultural integration rose up from the ashes of the Second World War. We are indebted for this initial idea to the open-mindedness and intuition of great men like Monnet, Schuman, Adenauer, and De Gasperi. Working together, Europeans sought the unity lost and never regained after the fall of Charlemagne's great empire. In the delicate postwar period, when our countries had to return to their normal business amid the material and moral destruction of the greatest conflict that ever struck our continent, France demonstrated far-sightedness and sensitivity for which it deserves Europe's eternal gratitude. Although one of the victors, it looked to the future and advocated a new alliance based on shared aims, peace, solidarity, and political and economic integration. This is something we should not forget. Apart from our common cultural roots, we know that France and Europe are indissolubly linked. France is a vital part of the historical process of building the European Union. This is why Italy attaches such importance to this great neo-Latin nation's role in our common endeavour. However, there is a more profound reason for the high regard in which we hold this country: France's presence is a guarantee that our cultural tradition and our deeply held values will have the role they deserve in the creation of the new Europe.

It has often been said that Europe is the child of the Latin and Germanic cultures, and without them Europe would not be the same. Our national past, our common cultural history and our traditional affinities are an important heritage for Europe and it is in Europe that they will be able to find new vigour and strength. Besides, only an awareness of our past can help us to build the future. When Europe enlarges to include the great cultural tradition of the Slav nations, it will be all the more important for none of our common identity to be lost and for everything to coexist in a higher and more vigorous synthesis.

All around us on the frontiers of our continent and the frontiers of Italy itself, there are pressures from new realities, new peoples and new forces.

(2) History is again on the move in Europe and on its frontiers. We can experience these developments either with a siege mentality or as a great challenge. I believe that, partly because of the strength it derives from our civilization, Europe can and must be a credible partner and mediator in these new worlds, which have finally returned to history. Over the centuries, we have contended with many new realities that appeared from beyond our seas, and we have consistently forged new relationships with peoples and countries who differed from ourselves. The tradition that we have inherited has dominated history for this reason – this ability of ours to lead and to set an example to other peoples and races. Without the profound values of tolerance and respect for human rights, which found their highest expression precisely in France, the world would be less civilized and Europe would be the poorer and less able to meet the demands of the future. This is another reason and a finer one for pushing ahead with pride on the fast track to integration.

We have all worked hard to ensure that our countries meet the Maastricht parameters. Economic and monetary union, which had once seemed impossible, is now a reality. Nothing will ever be the same again. The integration of national currencies into a single one is leading to a great integration of national economic policies. Anything that occurs in one of the countries in the monetary union will have immediate and direct significance for the others.

(3) The European Union will have to broaden its agenda to address welfare policies. It will be a complex transition, just as complex as the route we have already covered. But this transition will have to be carried through. In this century, Europeans created the welfare state, a great contribution to humanity as a whole. Precisely for this reason, the European Union cannot look on welfare policies as something almost marginal or even unrelated to our common development, as it has until now. The creation of compatible systems of social security and industrial and working relations is the next challenge we have chosen to meet. Global competition and the need to hold firm to the objectives of monetary integration are forcing our countries to rethink our social security systems. Each country is faced with difficult choices. All of them are encountering similar difficulties and tend to give similar responses, albeit against the backcloth of their specific national histories.

The time is now right to turn what is currently a national debate into a European debate. It is time for Europeans to think as Europeans about these issues as well as others. We have to understand that in future our efforts cannot be restricted or even dominated by our own national histories. This is because European integration is about to speed up considerably.

The first challenge for tomorrow's Union will be the harmonization of our various national systems of the social security and industrial relations, which will have to comply with the restrictions imposed by international competition on the European system. That tomorrow is almost upon us, knocking at our door and affecting millions and millions of Europeans. We would indeed be in trouble if we came to this appointment with history unprepared and unable to address these questions with wisdom, responsibility, a sense of timing and a generous attitude towards each other. We would be running the risk of turning our fellow citizens away from Europe. France is a nation that is particularly close to us on this question.

(4) The entire process of building Europe will inevitably and necessarily speed up after monetary union. Fortunately, European integration is well advanced in matters affecting both business and the individual. European citizens have now acquired a clear awareness that nationality of a Union member

state translates into increased rights of citizenship and a greater
sense of security. We are determined to make every effort to
implement fully the regulations currently in force and promote
our common freedom and security. Italy is profoundly convinced that 'European Union' must mean an increasing sense
of belonging to a shared legal framework of liberty, security
and common citizenship. This is why Italy increased its commitment to full membership of the Schengen Agreement.[1] We
know that the security of one country means security for them
all. We know that we too, like all the other countries, have a
duty both to our citizens and to all the citizens of the Union.
For this reason, we are determined to fulfil the agreements and
fully implement the joint regulations, even when this could
impose considerable burdens on us in terms of guarding our
frontiers and turning away illegal immigrants humanely but
firmly. However, precisely because we attach such importance
to the very notion of European citizenship, we believe that it
is right to speed up the process of creating and strengthening
the Union's political institutions.

(5) On the question of European institutions too, Italy and
France have adopted the same positions in recent times. We
started our political project with the economy. We pursued it
with determination towards increasingly close integration, which
also involved, as I have just pointed out, a major important
extension to the rights enjoyed by our citizens. But without
doubt, the time has now come to go beyond this, to look
further ahead and to equip our project with stronger instruments and institutions. This great question of strengthening
the Union's institutions was discussed in greater depth in
Amsterdam,[2] but we still have not found a completely satisfactory solution. We have to be able to make this leap. Monetary
integration demands it, and so does greater co-ordination over
economic and welfare policies.
   Monetary union could be achieved with the Community's
existing political institutions. But would we be able to handle
the changes that integration will bring without a more robust
institutional framework? It is not only *economic reasons* that
are pushing us towards a strengthening of our institutions –
there is also the question of *citizenship*. An area of European

citizenship is already a concrete legal reality. There is already a European legal corpus that regulates much of our economic and labour relations, and profoundly influences our domestic legislation. With complete freedom of circulation of goods, people and capital, decisions taken in all the countries of the Union have become increasingly important for all Europeans. The rights and duties that accompany national citizenship are therefore becoming increasingly unsatisfactory and there is a pressing need to strengthen the political rights and duties relating to membership of the Union.

There is a third and final important reason that obliges us to move more rapidly towards strengthening our common institutions. The European Union cannot be a closed system, because this would be in conflict with its original nature and its founding ideals. It is obliged by its very nature and its historical vocation to be heedful of requests by European countries to join. Equally, it is becoming very clear that it has to address the question of where it is to position itself and how it is to act on the international stage. The re-emergence of many European countries that for decades were kept at the margins of our continent's existence and their return to the mainstream have forced us in recent years to examine the question of enlarging the Union.

(6) This enlargement is in many ways inscribed in the genetic code of the project we gave life to fifty years ago. The European Council of Luxembourg (December 1997) was called on to decide which countries should be invited to the negotiating table.[3] Assessing the progress made by each candidate was a test of political foresight. It would have been a mistake to cultivate feelings of exclusion. Stronger Community institutions are the only necessary condition for this enlargement to proceed on a sound footing. We cannot grasp the historical opportunity posed by enlargement without strengthening the Union's institutional framework.

There is another reason why we have a historical duty to strengthen the Union. On our national borders, the borders of our Europe, there are tensions and dangers to the peace and security of millions of people. We Europeans can and should approach the problems that this poses in a responsible and united manner. We have a duty to take on a role commensurate with our economic strength, our geographical position, our moral values and the duty of every person to bring peace and justice to the conflicts that afflict humanity. We Europeans can no longer avoid the need for a foreign policy that is more proactive than in the past. The Union must adopt a common defence policy. We need to assert and consolidate a European defence and security identity within the context of the Atlantic Alliance.

The time has therefore come for us to rethink both the role of France and Italy and the role of the Union. Italy clearly opted for this more responsible stance when it asked to lead the multinational protection force in Albania,[4] which received spontaneous support above all from Mediterranean countries or countries most concerned with Mediterranean problems, such as France, Spain, Greece, Romania, Turkey, Austria, Denmark, Belgium and Slovenia. France too sent a large contingent, the second-largest after the Italian one, and it did so with generosity and foresight for which both Italy and I personally are very grateful. In any event, Albania has taught us that we Europeans now have to take on our share of responsibility.

(7) Today, we need to think and take our foreign policy decisions primarily from a European perspective. We have a duty to guarantee the defence of our citizens and a stable peace in a region of the world that is close to us, while maintaining our alliances and historical links. Our Union must be concerned with balanced development. This too is an important lesson provided by our common history. We know that in order to defend peace, we need to be ready to meet our own responsibilities. France has taught the world that it is right and possible to reconcile the great tradition of welcoming foreigners and other civilizations with the defence of one's own principles and values. We in the European Union must make the great tradition of *accueil* or warm hospitality our common heritage, opening ourselves to the world and at the same time asking the world to respect our values, our decisions and our plans. As Europeans we are heirs to a civilization that has known for centuries that no person, nation or continent can cut itself off from the rest of the world. We must return to

doing what for many centuries our countries were good at doing: attracting the best minds and being the adoptive land of the freest spirits. Our very ability to compete in research and advanced technologies depends on this, and consequently so does our future.

Notes

1   On 14 June 1985, the three Benelux countries (Belgium, Holland and Luxembourg), France and Germany met in Schengen, a small town in Luxembourg on the border with France and Germany, and signed an agreement to abolish gradually the controls on their common borders. On 19 June 1990, a convention was agreed on the means of applying this agreement. On 27 November 1990, an agreement was signed with Italy, to which a specific protocol was appended which regulated its application. Similar agreements were concluded with Spain and Portugal in 1991, with Greece in 1992, with Austria in 1995, and with Denmark, Finland and Sweden in 1996. The whole set of agreements, which has given rise to what is called the Schengen System, provides for the realization of the principle of free movement of people and the gradual abolition of border controls along common borders. A protocol appended to the Treaty of Amsterdam makes provision for the Schengen agreements to become part of the rules of the European Union, although they would only be applicable to the states that signed the Schengen Convention.

2   Reference has already been made in ch. 1 to the essential points in Treaty of Amsterdam. A brief and clear explanation of its results can be found in M. Emerson, *Redrawing the Map of Europe* (London: Macmillan Press, 1998). See esp. ch. 6, 'The institutions'.

3   Reference was also made to this argument in ch. 1, and in particular n. 13 gives a brief summary of the European Councils that led to the decisions on enlargement in the second half of the 1990s. Again Emerson's book (n. 2 above) goes into greater depth.

4   Operation 'Alba', which was promoted by Italy and implemented between April and August 1998 with the approval of the UN Security Council, involved the deployment of about 7,000 soldiers from Italy, France, Greece, Turkey, Spain, Romania, Austria, Denmark, Belgium and Slovenia. It achieved its purpose of halting Albania's descent into anarchy, started the recovery of control over the country by the authorities, and laid the foundations for a return to democratic dialogue and social and economic development.

3

In search of Europe's soul

In many ways, Italy today is a 'new' Italy that has rediscovered a belief in its powers of renewal, and faith in its own hard work. It has undertaken its own rebirth with determination. Building on the memory of its past, Italy now has hope in its future within Europe. Indeed, Europe was a vital reference point for the policies of the government over which I presided. The European project responds to one of Italy's profound desires. In Italy we want to make our own contribution based on our civilization, its economic and social development, our political stability and our culture.

I will approach this idea of Europe's 'soul' from four different perspectives: the founding fathers and the present generation; the Italian contribution to European integration; the Christian tradition and the European ideal; and the current challenges to civilization.

(1) We are one of the countries that gave birth to the post-war idea of Europe. The founding fathers of Europe left a great moral and political legacy: the idea of European integration as the basis for stability, peace and civilization among peoples – Europe as the guarantor of peace. Our parents' generation felt that the continent in which, against its very spirit, some of the greatest catastrophes in history had taken place, could and should constitute a bulwark for the peace and development of peoples, reviving its enlightened and Christian spirit.

The European community that was born in Rome just over forty years ago out of the horrors of war and totalitarianism, represented a clear break with the previous few years of European history. In the first place, it was necessary to eradicate the scourge of *economic nationalism*, which had long been the principal cause of conflicts and wars between European nations. The founding fathers started with the idea that free trade would be the means of overcoming the risk of economic nationalism.

The second element was to encourage civil society to become more independent and accept the central role of the market and free competition in generating social well-being, while state intervention should be confined to providing social security for the weaker members of society and guaranteeing their rights. The ideals of liberty and equality were achieved creatively through the political transition from the centrality of the state to the primacy of the individual citizen.

Third, they opted for democracy as the best way of achieving political union in Europe. They envisaged a Europe created by the free choice of its citizens and not by the strength of its armies. It is particularly important to reaffirm those decisions and values, in the wake of the events of 1989 and the end of the cold war. These profound changes mean that we Europeans are neither dominators nor dominated. We are neither outcasts nor conquerors. We finally find ourselves at a crossroads in history where fully democratic models of the balance of power are possible both in domestic and in international terms. It is particularly important to reaffirm those values now that Europe has become a great economic reality and an economic point of reference on a global scale. We should bear these democratic values in mind in our present efforts to achieve a single European currency. Indeed, by striving for economic convergence, we are responding to the need to ensure lasting stability and development of our civilization along peaceful and *humanitarian* lines. Indeed, to maintain that economic development is divorced from or unconnected to moral and political development is to deny the European tradition and its impact on humanity. It is precisely because of this profound relationship between economic rationalism and ethical rationalism that Europe must be rigorous and responsible in economic and financial matters.

Another formidable challenge – but also a great opportunity – is the globalization of markets, and the new ways in which production is organized. Nor can we continue to ignore the extraordinary process whereby democratic values are being espoused by countries that for too long have been excluded from European history. For this reason, we have initiated a process, which will ultimately see the European Union further enlarged and with it the area of freedom and affluence that we have enjoyed for decades.

(2) Italy is strongly committed to contributing to the creation of Europe. During the period when I was head of government, our country was guided by six objectives.

(a) *Full participation from the beginning in the third phase of Economic and Monetary Union.* This clearly meant putting our own house in order rather than acting on the international front. Great effort had already been expended. We intensified and broadened these efforts and this paid off when we joined the single currency.[1]

(b) *Joining Schengen.* With the final approval of the law protecting personal data and the implementation of all the measures for effective border controls, we fulfilled all the obligations laid down by the agreement on the Schengen Information System, and on 26 October 1997 Italy became a full member.

(c) *Revision of the Maastricht Treaty.* In accordance with the Inter-Governmental Conference set up under our presidency at the European Council in Turin, we undertook to strengthen the Community institutions, by extending the areas covering common policies, reducing the areas reserved for the jurisdiction of the member states, and establishing a common foreign and security policy in which defence would play a significant role. The Amsterdam Summit made it possible to make some progress, particularly towards enlarging the Union. We are convinced that precisely because of the prospect of an enlarged Union, we shall have to pursue the business of strengthening our institutions, which was left largely unfinished in Amsterdam.

More specifically, changes are required to make the decision-making process more effective and increase the policy areas covered by majority voting, thus reducing the number of areas where decisions require the assent of all the member states.

Under this process, every citizen, political grouping and state is called upon to acknowledge the existence of a 'common European interest' that exceeds, incorporates and fulfils the 'common interest of each nation'. We are, in fact, convinced of the profound impact that Europe will have on all the parties joining and using the Community framework.

(d)   *Support for the enlargement process.* We have always considered this to be of strategic importance, both economically and for international and domestic security. Welcoming countries that were always part of our common European identity into the fold of the European Union means closing, once and for all, the chapter of our continent's artificial division. It is now possible to launch the general process of 'Europeanizing Europe'. Pope John Paul II reminded us of this in his appeal at Gniezno on 3 June 1997, when at the tomb of St Adalbert and in front of the heads of state of central and eastern Europe, he called upon Europeans 'to commit themselves resolutely to constructive co-operation in order to create peace among themselves and around themselves. They cannot', he exclaimed, 'leave out any nation, however weak, from the totality of what they are building.'

(e)   *Dialogue between the Middle East and the Mediterranean.* We chose to concentrate our foreign policy on these two areas in order to demonstrate our European responsibility and the need for our presence because of our geographical position and shared heritage of civilization. Responsibility and involvement in the dialogue means promoting Europe's solidarity with other peoples. It is a responsibility that history itself demands, and it matches our own particular vocation. Italy has an essential role in the new Europe. Indeed it would not be possible to have a Europe that was deprived of the part most closely linked to its Latin tradition.

(f)   *Social dimensions to Community policies.* Giving economic
policies more of a social dimension certainly does not
mean that employment policies slip out of the hands of
individual member states. It is only at European level
that we can deal with issues of Europe-wide importance.
Completion of Economic and Monetary Union must therefore allow us to free up resources and use them for growth
and the creation of new jobs. With current levels of
unemployment (over 10 per cent almost everywhere in
Europe), too many young people cannot achieve their
potential and society as a whole is deprived of valuable
human resources. In his first social encyclical *Laborem
exercens*, John Paul II warns that 'man is a creature who
needs to work'. If this is true, then not only is he the sum
of his own labours – and so his labour should be neither
exploited nor alienated – but also he achieves his dignity
as a man through honest labour. So when jobs are in short
supply, those who cannot find work find their identity as
human beings and as citizens seriously threatened.

In past decades, Europe has taught the world how to reconcile development with solidarity, efficiency with equity. Today
we face the challenge of redesigning our socio-economic model,
which is now unsuited to resolving the dualism between those
who are within the labour market and therefore protected,
and those who are excluded, struggling to get in and unpro-
tected. A just society is built upon the two equally essential
and interrelated principles of *solidarity* and *subsidiarity*, which
according to Christian social teaching demonstrate that man is
both a unique individual and a social being. Only by striving
for solidarity and subsidiarity can we achieve a greater degree
of justice and liberty, otherwise our democracies will become
mechanisms for balancing different selfish interests.

This is the position we have reached in relation to reform of
the welfare state. I would say that it is the principal area in
which European countries must help each other. Above all
else, political will is required if we are to respond to people's
needs, and this can only be forthcoming at a European level.
Anything else would only be a 'competitive' lowering of standards in relation to both social policy and citizens' rights.

(3) We can never be grateful enough to John Paul II for having asked (I would almost say 'forced') the Christian churches on our continent to reflect on the relationship between the spirit of Europe and Christianity. Faced with different historical needs, he followed through to their conclusion thoughts that had already undergone an incontestable cultural development under Paul VI. According to him, attention to 'supreme ethical and juridical principles' required the Church to be committed to Europe, in the conviction that 'the Christian message interprets man's profound needs in this case as in others'. It is a duty that the Church and Christians shoulder in accordance with 'the centuries-long history of Europe itself, which has already experienced a common consciousness in the past and a unity permeated with Christian values'.[2]

In the case of John Paul II, the reference to the values of European humanism takes on a topical relevance. Enlargement of the European Union cannot really take place without building a spiritual bridge between the peoples of eastern and western Europe. This reflects the Slav pope's historical awareness and spiritual restlessness. Europe cannot be understood without its Christian roots. Christianity has left its mark on Europe, and that mark is still there. The different cultures of the European nations and their art, literature and ways of thinking share a common nourishment, which is fed upon by believers and non-believers alike. The diversity of European nations and peoples has incorporated the Christian way of life. This is why we have to rediscover both pluralism and a shared inspiration to experience the ideal of Europe. Being aware of this, those of us who are European Catholic democrats are inspired to revive fully the idea of Europe: a political, cultural and economic idea, and a spiritual idea as well. Without this awareness and without the Christian tradition that supports it, there is a real risk that new barriers – social, cultural and spiritual – will rise up in place of the old ones. If this were to happen, we would have failed in our aim of reuniting Europe and creating the pluralist, transnational, transcultural and spiritually inspired amalgam, that seemed – perhaps naïvely – well within our grasp following the events of 1989.

Europe is a continent of many national communities, each with its own physiognomy, its own culture and its own language.

It is a Europe of people and of peoples. It is composed of economic, political and social identities that complement each other in a vital manner. The challenge that faces us as Europeans and as European Christians is that of helping them all to progress while maintaining their fertile interrelations. Europe was never, at any stage of its development, merely a convenience or a necessity. At every stage in the development of Europe, there was a profound connection between the 'European cause' and its 'Christian roots'. This is why the great project of European unity revives 'the harmony between a great political design and the general principles of man and society'.[3]

Europe's destiny is not inherently Eurocentric, but one of universality. It should therefore reassert its role as the 'beacon for world civilization'. This is possible and sustainable as long as its historical memory goes back beyond the ideals of the last few centuries and, while still encompassing them, rediscovers its religious roots (and not just its Christian ones). Such a role could eventually revive the Christian soul of Europe which is the basis for unity. This revival must not be perceived as a new plan for Christianity, but rather as a return to the conviction expressed in the Letter to Diognetus: 'what the soul is to the body, Christians are to the world' (we might add: 'of Europe'). It is precisely this dual consciousness of commitment to religious faith and full political responsibility, and having to aspire to a new cultural unity through a debate over ideals that gives us renewed vigour, an identity and a role to play. Instilling a soul in today's Europe means helping to shape its conscience.

'What we are being called upon to build', Cardinal Carlo Maria Martini pointed out,

> is a Europe of the spirit, by rediscovering and re-advocating those values that moulded it throughout its long history: the dignity of the human being, the sacred nature of life, the central role of the family, the importance of education, freedom of thought, speech and the expression of one's own convictions and religion, legal protection of individuals and groups, the co-operation of all people in the common good, work as a personal and a social good, and the authority of the state subject to the law and to reason and limited by the rights of individuals and peoples.[4]

All values, it should be said, that have been asserted thanks to the multiplicity of cultural traditions.

(4) Because of its spiritual richness, Christianity inspires us to meet the challenges facing tomorrow's Europe, through a stronger European consciousness and an awareness of Europe's role in the world. What are these challenges that we will have to face?

Reconciling man with nature

This is what the First European Ecumenical Assembly, held in Basel in 1989, called 'safeguarding the creation'.

Acknowledging 'otherness' and the ability of cultures to live together

This means the mutual acceptance among Europeans of their cultural diversity. Europe is currently experiencing a resurgence of frenzied and tragic forms of nationalism, and an assertion of self-interested and closed mindsets. The result has been another war in the heart of Europe. As Europeans we were slow to accept our political responsibilities in relation to these recent events in the Balkans. A Europe, with its wide variety of traditions, cultures, ethnic groups and religions, requires understanding, warmth and integration.

Understanding anew our historical past

This is particularly important in view of our own tragic history. In this century, in this continent, and at the very heart of Europe, one of the most terrible catastrophes in human history occurred: the Holocaust. The world was fully entitled to expect greater spiritual resistance of Christ's followers, and if we were not sufficiently vigilant and in some cases were involved in *inhuman behaviour*, it is because for centuries we allowed the growth of an unjustifiable anti-Semitic tradition, which was completely foreign to the Christianity taught in the New Testament.

The Holocaust took place before and during a war, in whose iniquity and evil we Italians have our share of the blame, and for which we must ask forgiveness. For the sake of those victims, whom we cannot and must not forget, we should show a great sense of responsibility as men and women of spirit, as governments and as peoples, in eliminating all forms of racism, xenophobia and anti-Semitism. There can be no Europe, if ethnic cleansing, nationalism, racial superiority and anti-Semitism again become words that can be uttered and are uttered. The new Europe must develop fully the ethic of law and the protection of fundamental rights, to the point of taking severe measures and harsh sanctions against those countries that are responsible for discrimination against persons, peoples, cultures and religions. There is no place for them in Europe.

Welcoming diversity

This means displaying an openness to other peoples and cultures, welcoming foreigners and refugees in accordance with Community regulations, and openness to the spiritual wealth of peoples from other continents.

Increasing our sense of responsibility

This represents a kind of turning-point in our anthropological approach. Today, there is again a growing tendency to reject responsibility, accept no guilt and suspend morality. It is something like the death of reason. It is an extension of technological reasoning whereby 'I am always and only my own experiment', a power that is exercised beyond good and evil. It is not like that for those of us who put our Christian faith at the root of our existence, and this faith helps us to point out all the risks in this development.

(5) In one of the finest passages of contemporary thought, which we owe to the philosopher and theologian Romano

Guardini, an Italian who has taught in Germany, these danger-ous features of the postmodern age are described as follows:

> The modern age congratulates itself on the fact that it bases the norms of technology on its usefulness to man's prosperity, but it ignores the destruction that this lack of scruples produces. I believe that times are approaching in which we will express ourselves differently. Mankind, the protagonist, knows that ultimately it is not a question of utility or prosperity, but of dominion: dominion in the extreme meaning of the word. Man is attempting to grasp the elements of both nature and human existence at the same time, and this means endless possibilities for finding and constructing positive solutions to many of the most acute problems facing the planet, starting with hunger, but also including those concerning its destruction, particularly where human nature is the cause. Here our relationship with nature becomes a matter of decisive choice.

If we apply this thought to the current development of technological sectors such as biology, genetics, communications and armaments, we can see the opportunities and the risks that current changes will bring. But the challenge that we face is not one of rejecting or attempting to obstruct these develop-ments, since this would not be possible and it would be foolish to think it might be. It is a question of attempting to regulate these developments, to have power over this power. For this to be possible, we need to bring about a great moral revolution, increasing our awareness and hence our sense of responsibility, and applying our conscience with greater wisdom.

Notes

1   A more detailed description of Italy's convergence towards Eco-nomic and Monetary Union can be found in ch. 4. For the other principal developments, the reader is simply referred here to the chapters concerned with economic and institutional questions.
2   Paul VI, *Speech to the Audience at the Conference of the European Movement*, 9 November 1963.
3   Paul VI, *Letter to Cardinal A. Casaroli*, 25 July 1975.
4   This was the address to the Symposium of the European Parlia-ment on the occasion of the sixteenth centenary of the death of St Ambrose (Strasbourg, 17 September 1997).

4

Europe in an interdependent world

(1) Everyone agrees that the advent of the euro will bring changes of historic importance, but also that it is extremely difficult to predict what these changes will be. Perhaps not everyone is aware that some historic changes had *already taken place* in Europe and in Italy in particular, long before the formal advent of the euro on 1 January 1999.

During the 1990s, monetary and financial policy in Europe and Italy changed quite dramatically. There have been similar changes in other non-European industrialized countries. Now we enjoy low inflation and reduced budget deficits, and this will continue for some time, supported by the Maastricht Treaty and the European Central Bank. However, there is another equally important change: a profound conviction among all European citizens that this new environment is essential for our economic prosperity. This conviction is particularly strong in Italy. Some believe that this acceptance by Italy of the new regime was a cosmetic operation with the sole aim of obtaining admission to the third phase of monetary union.[1] Nothing could be further from the truth. Italy is now one of the European countries where the public understands best how essential it is to have responsible financial targets and macroeconomic stability. Just as it is claimed that German hyperinflation immunized the Germans against the harmful effects of monetary instability, the excesses of the 1980s and 1990s have immunized Italians against the harmful effects of financial and monetary policies that are too casual in their approach.

(2) But the European revolution of the 1990s means much more than this. Now we have free movement of capital and labour everywhere. The Schengen Agreement has eliminated passport controls at frontiers. The tariff barriers to the circulation of goods and services in Europe have all disappeared. Europe is a huge single market of goods, services and production factors, in all senses, and not just rhetorically. The euro will help the single market to operate even more smoothly and will promote competition. We should highlight the benefits that will result from this encouragement of competition in terms of efficient private enterprises and sensible public sector policies. We have already begun to notice some of the beneficial effects. Maximization of the share values has become a very important result for the large public limited companies in Europe and particularly in Italy. Restructuring is proceeding fast, especially in the service sector. Privatizations are being carried through more and more rapidly and will continue in the whole of Europe and in Italy. And indeed it should be pointed out that these revolutionary – and crucial – changes preceded the advent of the euro.

There are those in the United States who greeted the European adventure with diffidence. In effect, we have to acknowledge that it is extremely difficult to predict and assess all the long-term implications that will derive from the creation of the euro. However, the critics perhaps do not realize the strength of the foundations on which the new European currency is being built.

(3) Economic and Monetary Union is an act of faith in Europe, the culmination of a long process initiated many years ago with the creation of the Common Market and subsequently the Single Market in which there is complete freedom of movement of goods, services, people and capital. But EMU also represents a challenge in the wider context of the world economy. The 'euro zone' or 'Euroland' covers the eleven countries in which the euro was born, and that is a good beginning for keeping up with the United States, the country with which there is and will continue to be the fiercest competition in international markets. Many sources agree that the gross domestic product for the euro zone is about 80 per cent of the GDP of the United States[2] (it follows that the GDP for the fifteen

member states as a whole will be even greater than that of the United States) and that Euroland is a considerable trading power.[3]

If we move on from the overall picture to a more detailed comparison, what differences do we find between the euro zone and the United States? The first is the ratio between domestic consumer demand, investments and GDP, or in other words a different incidence of foreign trade. Indeed, the euro zone pro- · duces a current account surplus on its balance of payments of about 2 per cent of GDP, whereas the United States' current account deficit is over 1 per cent. Trade in goods between the two areas, which since 1996 has been once again in the euro zone's favour, should be sustained in particular by the surpluses in Germany and Italy (although globalization will probably have the effect of reducing these surpluses).

The second difference is the evolution of budget deficits in the two areas. Since 1998, the United States has been showing a budget surplus.[4] However, the euro zone has a budget deficit that is less than 3 per cent of GDP and should further diminish in the coming years as a result of the convergence process imposed by the Stability and Growth Pact in the wake of the Maastricht Treaty. Moreover the ratio between public debt and GDP will be greater in the European area: 74.5 per cent of GDP, as against 60 per cent in the United States. This phenomenon has a twin significance, however: on the one hand, it restricts budget policies in the European area, but on the other, the quantity of European government securities in circulation will tend to equal that of American ones, and will help to make the market wider and more fluid, and therefore attractive to international investors. In 1999, however, the greatest difference continued to be the unemployment rate, which was unlikely to drop below the 11 per cent mark in the euro zone, while in the United States it was predicted to stay below the 5 per cent mark.

(4) It is therefore a priority to return the European economy to a phase of strong and prolonged growth. The recent macro-economic stability will prove particularly significant in achieving this aim. The Maastricht Treaty was a great act of justice towards the young and future generations. Imposing limits on budget deficits and public debt prevents national governments from

burdening future generations with costs, as they have done in the past. The fight against inflation and the substantial reduction in interest rates has created the conditions for a new cycle of investments. Exchange-rate stability has improved business confidence and increased the value and effectiveness of real competition between enterprises, since it has not been distorted by the devaluation of individual national currencies. It is my firm belief that macroeconomic stability is a fundamental requirement for long-term economic development. And here, the considerable reduction in interest rates in all the EU member states, including Italy, should be considered a great triumph and essential for success in fighting unemployment.

The experience of recent years has shown that there is no distinction between 'phase one' and 'phase two' of an economic policy. The campaign to sort out budget problems has created the conditions for recovery in the whole of Europe, and not just in the short term. At the same time, measures of a structural nature are being implemented in the member states to promote development that is increasingly necessary now that it is no longer possible to resort to increased public borrowing and currency devaluation.

There seems to be a general principle inspiring the new Europe that could be summarized as: 'Let's get Europe back to work.' With its single currency, Europe will have a common monetary policy at supranational level. There will also be a restriction on the use of expansionist financial policies, given the constraints imposed on public finances. Consequently we shall be seeing a greater use of policies aimed at stimulating private business initiatives, within the context of increasing liberalization of the European economy and, more generally, of the global economy.

(5) If, as has been said, the current changes in Europe are revolutionary, those in Italy are even more so. Over a period of a few years, it has managed to do the following:[5]

- cut its *deficit* from 6.8 per cent of GDP in 1996 to 2.7 per cent at the end of 1997 (remember that membership of the single currency from 1 January 1999 was subject to satisfying the rules laid down by the Maastricht Treaty by 31 December 1997);

- reduce *inflation* from 4.6 per cent in 1996 to 1.6 per cent at the end of 1997;
- reduce *long-term interest rates*: they were showing an average of about 6.9 per cent in the twelve-month period ending in December 1997, and therefore a lower average than the reference figure of 7.8 per cent established in relation to the three countries with the greatest stability;
- rapidly lower the ratio between *public debt* and GDP: this was due to the combined effect of the high primary surplus and the reduction in interest rates;
- re-enter the European Monetary System (EMS) on 25 November 1996: after that the lira stayed very close to the *central parities* set with the other EMS currencies and the reference exchange rate of 990 lire against the German mark;
- reform the *public pension system* and lay the foundations for a *private* pension system that will become increasingly important;
- *liberalize and privatize* many economic sectors, including the banking, food and energy sectors: proceeds from the privatization programme implemented by the Treasury in the period 1994–7 amounted to over 65,000 billion lire (about 40 billion US dollars), of which 37,900 billion lire were for 1997 alone; during this period, it achieved the largest privatization programme ever undertaken in Europe; in 1998 Italy again came out top of the privatization league with proceeds of 13.62 billion dollars;[6]
- simplify many aspects of the *civil service* and create *regional autonomy* by decentralizing taxation and responsibility for expenditure;
- simplify and reform various aspects of the *tax system*.

The implications of these changes are far-reaching and lasting. They have placed Italy in a position from which it will be able to draw enormous benefits from the opportunities and challenges arising from the euro and its new competitive environment. An overall assessment of the Italian performance against the convergence criteria shows that we meet Maastricht requirements. Careful examination reveals a kind of paradigm for budget recovery that was followed over the two-year period

1996–8: an economy with a high budget deficit cannot lower taxes before permanently cutting expenditure; and expenditure, in turn, can only be reduced structurally by taking measures affecting the civil service and the right of citizens to receive public funds. This is precisely what we did: the exceptional increase in taxation in 1997 helped to buy time in order to carry through a wide range of reforms (the civil service, tax collection, the labour market and welfare spending) which will come into force over time. These reforms will either cut expenditure or widen the tax base, thus reducing fiscal pressure.

(6) In any event, monetary union is only one part of the wider process of European integration. The challenges that await us range from strengthening European institutions to enlarging the Union to include eastern Europe, to mention just two.

Italy is fulfilling a new role in this situation. We have realized that, in an increasingly interdependent world, stability and prosperity cannot be nurtured exclusively with the instruments of national economic policy, given that the health of the global economy on which many of our industries rely also depends on the stability of the international system. Awareness of this process is an important development in Italy's attitude to foreign affairs. Although Italy has changed considerably in recent years, the basic premises of its foreign policy remain unchanged. Indeed, our two continuing international priorities, the *transatlantic* and *European* orientation of our foreign policy, have, if anything, been reinforced. It is not our intention to change this policy, but rather to pursue it further, given that Italy can count on a more robust economy and a more reliable political situation.

Whereas Italy kept a low profile during the cold war because of its weak and vulnerable domestic situation, it is now ready to take on the responsibilities that go with its stronger position. But this does not mean that we will allow ourselves to be seduced by an Italian version of 'mini-Gaullism' or the old policy of economic isolationism. We are conscious that our problems are the same as those that afflict our allies, and that they can only be resolved within a multilateral framework.

With these considerations in mind, we have tried to make our policy more credible and to ensure that our point of view is taken into account. If necessary, we are not afraid of taking on the primary responsibility, as happened in the case of Albania, but we remain convinced that, rather than trying 'to do it ourselves', it is perhaps better to take the initiative.

(7) Our foreign policy still centres on our transatlantic relations, which are the principal source of stability for the international system as a whole. Membership of NATO has been very important for Italy and has helped define the very identity of our republic since the war. This is why we believe that reforming NATO and updating its rules and operational methods are one of the most important issues we have to tackle. As far as international reform of NATO and its command structure are concerned, we supported the United States' efforts in the Mediterranean through the Allied Forces' Southern Command, because we consider the American presence to be the very essence of the Alliance.

The enlargement of NATO will allow us finally to overcome the anachronistic divisions of the cold war and increase the chances of peace in eastern and south-eastern Europe through the transition towards democracy and the market economy.[7] The difficulties and the costs that enlargement will bring will be worthwhile in terms of continental peace. I do not believe that this process will create problems with Russia. Indeed, if matters are not resolved, it is more likely that a situation of instability will emerge, given that politics, like physics, abhors a vacuum. The Russian problem really comes down to its internal disintegration, the collapse of its economic and political structures and the failure of a 'social compact' capable of holding the country together. From a strategic point of view, a role is emerging for a country that has been unjustly ignored and that will be the key to relations between the West and Russia. I am talking of the Ukraine, where the willingness of NATO and Russia to co-operate will be put to the test.

(8) As I have already said, Europe is the other great element of continuity in our foreign policy. The priority we put on monetary unification is a mark of this commitment of ours. Once again, European consciousness has profound roots in the Italian spirit, mainly because Italy's extraordinary economic

growth over the last forty years has been correctly interpreted as a product of European integration. This integration provided the right environment for industrial expansion.

Italy hopes to repeat this success by helping to bring about the Common Foreign and Security Policy (CFSP), since the national dimension is no longer sufficient. For this reason, we have been trying to make further progress in this direction since the Treaty of Amsterdam and we are observing with interest the current consolidation of the European defence industry,[8] which is a prerequisite for further integration. Even though the process of internationalizing the arms industry in European countries has, so far, been obstructed by a curious reticence or residual nationalism, all comparative technological assessments show that national defence industries in Europe do not have a future.

Italy could contribute more to multilateral efforts to stabilize international politics, and it will. Moreover, its economy has industrialized over recent decades and is now one of the seven greatest economic powers in the world. Italy will play its rightful role within G7, the forum for these economic powers.

(9) I have just mentioned Italy's support for the enlargement of both NATO and the European Union to include the east European countries. We have proposed a *rapprochement* with Romania and Slovenia, which would enlarge the area of peace to include the troubled Balkan region. Moreover, the importance of Bulgaria should not be underestimated. The importance of this region for Italy is exemplified by historical links that go back to the Habsburg Empire, when, for instance, the Trieste-based company Assicurazioni Generali did half of its business with eastern Europe. Today this tradition has been revived by our small and medium-sized enterprises, whose investments and business activities in eastern Europe have grown exponentially in recent years. There are, for example, over 6,000 small Italian companies operating in Romania, which shows that eastern Europe and the Balkans are a particular strength in our future economic and trading policy.

Italy was one of the first countries to contribute to the stabilization force in Bosnia, in spite of the doubts expressed by those who feared the historical implications of deploying Italian forces in the former Yugoslavia. Faced with the degeneration of the Albanian situation, Italy organized a multinational force in spite of the lukewarm response from NATO and the European Union and a bitter parliamentary dispute that brought my government to the brink of resignation. Today, Italy is sincerely committed to the contact group's attempts at mediation and to the non-governmental organizations dealing with the situation in Kosovo.

We are also aware of the vital importance of our country's southern front. The Mediterranean holds great opportunities,[9] because of its traditional status as a channel of communication between Europe and Asia, and it is proving to be a developing region that can offer high returns on investments from the developed parts of Europe. Furthermore, southern Italy will only reach high levels of prosperity through the establishment of a large Euro-Mediterranean economic zone. The stability of the Mediterranean region does not only concern Italy. It is a region of strategic importance for the whole of Europe and the Middle East, and I am certain it is also significant for the United States.

If we look at the wider picture, we see that Italy has encouraged economic and political reforms in the former soviet republics of central Asia, just as we have encouraged the construction of other oil pipelines to minimize the risks arising from dependence on just one.

We are well aware of the great risks presented by the southern shores of the Mediterranean. Italy is probably the country most exposed to mass immigration, and it would be the first western European country to be hit by weapons of mass destruction in the event of an armed conflict. Italy has sent troops to the Persian Gulf area on two occasions: at the end of the eighties and during the Gulf War. Italy also contributed to peace initiatives in the Lebanon and Somalia.

In view of our history and our geographical position, we are perfectly aware that it is impossible to build a lasting peace in the region without gaining the consent of local populations. As I have already argued, it is not possible to push these problems aside and dismiss them as the 'clash of civilizations' that some people fear. These problems have historical origins and there are no easy answers. We need to commit ourselves to building lasting solutions.

(10) Italy has become more reliable and more in tune with its important democratic allies. It is a natural consequence of its revitalized economic and political condition, as well as the realization that it is a front-line state facing a wide front affected by crises extending from North Africa to the Balkans, and passing through the Middle East and central Asia. We cannot allow the new policies that are taking shape to lead us away from our European and Atlantic vocation, which is stronger than ever. Instead we must foster a new, deep-seated resolve to take an active part in resolving our common problems together with our allies. Unfortunately, after the cold war (and unlike our predecessors who, following great conflicts, came together at international conferences such as those in Vienna and Versailles), we did not have an opportunity to plan an international system. But, luckily, if we have enough courage, we have the means to achieve greater success than they did in building a more peaceful and prosperous world for ourselves and for our children.

Notes

1   The creation of Economic and Monetary Union in three phases had been proposed back in 1989 by the Committee to examine Economic and Monetary Union, which was presided over by Jacques Delors (the president of the Commission). It published the *Report on Economic and Monetary Union of the European Community* (June 1990), which formed the basis for the provisions of the Maastricht Treaty on this subject. The first phase, which commenced in July 1990 with the complete liberalization of movement of capital, required greater effort to maintain fixed parities within the EMS. The second phase, which commenced in 1994, focused on the creation of the European Monetary Institute (EMI) as the precursor for the European Central Bank (established in May 1998 at the time of choosing the eleven countries to participate in the euro). The third and final phase came on 1 January 1999 with the launch of the euro, once conversion rates between the euro and the eleven national currencies had been irrevocably fixed on 31 December 1998. Euro banknotes

and coins will only be introduced from January 2002, and in June of the same year, national banknotes and coins will be definitively withdrawn from circulation.

2   An initial assessment ('The European economy in 1998 and 1999', *European Business Cycle Analysis*, May 1998) calculated that Euroland's GDP for 1997 was 5,684.9 billion ecus as against the US figure of 7,127.6. A second one ('The international euro', 'Euro brief 5', *The Economist*, 14 November 1998) put the 1997 figure at 6,500 billion dollars as against 8,100 in the USA. Leaving aside the precise figures, the analysis provided in the previously mentioned 'Essential characteristics of the euro zone' published in the *ECB Monthly Bulletin* of January 1999 (see ch. 1) is of great interest. The share of the world's GDP in the euro zone in 1997 was 15% compared with 20.2% in the United States and 7.7% in Japan (the values were calculated assuming constant prices and exchange rates at parity purchasing power in 1997; 1990 prices for the euro zone).

3   These are the same three sources referred to in the previous note on GDP, providing data on the Euroland and US shares of international trade. The most recent analysis (see *ECB Monthly Bulletin*), shows that, at the end of 1997, exports of goods as percentages of GDP were 13.6% in the euro zone (excluding of course its internal trade) and 8.5% in the USA, whereas imports as percentages of GDP were 12% and 11.1% respectively. But perhaps the most significant statistic is the one for exports from each area as percentages of world exports: again at the end of 1997 and excluding internal trade in the euro zone, the percentages were 15.7% (Euroland) and 12.6% (USA). Europe's lead does not change even if you include Japan (7.7%).

4   This is effectively what happened: for the first time since 1969, the federal budget recorded a surplus of 69 billion dollars, which is 0.8% of US GDP (see *Economic Report of the President 1999*, Washington: February 1999).

5   Most of the following information was taken from the report *La convergenza dell'Italia verso l'Unione economica e monetaria*, which was drawn up at the beginning of 1998 by the General Directorate of the Treasury and the technical departments of the Bank of Italy. The report was published in *Vita Italiana*, an official publication of the Prime Minister's Office (no. 2/3, XLVIII, April 1998). For a qualitative analysis of the convergence process, see issue no. 3/98 of *Il Mulino*, which was entirely devoted to the European question following Italy's entry into the single currency.

6 The OECD ranked countries according to this criterion (for a preview of the report, see *Il Sole 24 Ore*, 7 March 1999, p. 3), and placed Italy in lead position for the second consecutive year. Moreover, Italy is in second place, just behind the United Kingdom, in the ranking for privatizations over the period 1990–8 (63.47 billion dollars as against 64.04). Although the two studies (the OECD one and the previously mentioned Convergence Report) are a little different methodologically, both are agreed on the extensive nature of Italy's privatization programme.

7 The Czech Republic, Poland and Hungary were invited to the NATO Summit in Madrid in June 1997, they joined the Alliance in December 1997, and became full members on 12 March 1999. Other countries in central Europe have applied to become members of the Alliance.

8 Recently, the most important developments in the defence industry have taken place in Great Britain and France. In the first case, the high-profile merger between British Aerospace (BAe) and General Electric Corporation (GEC Marconi) fought off another bid (the merger proposal between the German Daimler-Benz Aerospace and BAe). In France, the merger between the private group Lagardere-Matra and the publicly owned group Aerospatiale is worthy of note. The latter also has a 46% holding in Dassault. At European level there are several bilateral joint ventures involving Italian industry, such as Alenia-Marconi and Augusta-Westland, and some multilateral (BAe, Lagardere, Dasa and Finmeccanica) for space and missile projects. In the political and institutional fields, it is particularly significant that the British prime minister asserted the need for developing an independent European defence capacity, partly by incorporating the Western European Union (WEU) into the EU (a move that Great Britain had previously opposed). This has undoubtedly put defence back on the European agenda.

9 The Mediterranean's rebirth as a crossroads for international trade will be the subject of chs 5, 6 and 7.

Part II

Europe and the Mediterranean

5

Mediterranean countries and the European Union

(1) The introduction of the euro completes the third phase of European integration, following the formation of the Common Market and the Single Market. This and the arrival of the third millennium should induce us to reflect on the essential nature of Europe's role in the world. While the twentieth century has been called the 'American century', it is also true that we have lived through the 'European millennium'.

The Mediterranean fulfilled a fundamental role in the last millennium as the cradle of civilization and as a crossroads for trade. In spite of economic, political and religious differences, the Mediterranean basin has always been a place where cultures meet and join together, and this has allowed it to remain, as Fernand Braudel argues in his famous theory, a single and indivisible system where different cultures and peoples interact. In an era of increasing globalization and the affirmation of a transnational culture, this vocation and ability to fuse disparate elements together will be an asset and an opportunity for all the coutries that surround the Mediterranean.

(2) Twenty-five centuries ago, 'Europe' became more than just a name from mythology. Europe came to be divided from Asia along a tiny strip of sea on the fringe of the Mediterranean, then known as the Hellespont. Here the cultural distinction between Europe and Asia took form, almost as though it were the genetic code for the separation between East and West. This separation was based on both conflict and the need

for interaction. For the Greeks, Asia was no longer a group of Ionic cities, and had become the Persian Empire. As an ancient manuscript says, 'the sea separated Europe from Asia'.

Although the opposing identities originated in war, there has always been a need to appeal to a common foundation. In the tragedy, *The Persians*, Aeschylus experienced this contradiction most acutely. Together with awareness of the importance of the conflict, there was a supreme compassion for the human condition in general. Thus the drama of the defeated Persians takes on a greater significance than praise for the victors' military virtues. Just when the kingdom of Philip of Macedonia seemed to emerge as an embryonic European state, his son Alexander sought out a new but temporary fusion between East and West, and the sea was again closed over. These were the first cycles in the long history of the Mediterranean, which has united and separated peoples, cultures and states. It was a sea around which events affecting one group were to become inextricably linked with events affecting the others. In other words, the Mediterranean is primarily a specific idea of 'civilization'. The French historian Georges Duby reminds us that English pilgrims in the Middle Ages, who undertook the gruelling journey to visit St Peter's tomb, were not just in search of salvation for their souls. Charles Martel and Pépin the Short were not only in search of booty as they advanced along Narbonnese Gaul. Nor was this the sole motive that drove Charlemagne to cross the Pyrenees or to travel to Rome to claim the title of Augustus. It was the fascination of civilization that lured the knights of Burgundy and Champagne as far as Aragon, Castile and Portugal, the loyal supporters of the king of Germany to Emilia, Tuscany and Latium, and the Normans to Palermo and Bari. And then beyond the sea to Jerusalem, Damietta and Tunis. When Toledo was reconquered, the conquerors immersed themselves in the riches they found in its libraries and translated the texts that the Arabs had preserved by translating them from Greek. 'For the most part, the conquerors returned to their native lands completely seduced and vanquished themselves.' It was a repetition of what the Romans had said of themselves: that they had conquered Greece, but Greece had conquered them. Time and again, Europe, Asia and Africa have merged in the Mediterranean. The Mediterranean has produced an immense cycle of civilizations and has profoundly marked the world's culture by expanding to the Americas.

(3) Today we are witnessing the tumultuous development of Asia and the recovery of the Mediterranean's centrality: an economic, political and cultural centrality.

The importance of the Mediterranean for *communications* is in fact re-emphasized by recent trends in the world economy. The growing role of the Asian economy has shifted the main axis of international trade, which for four centuries has been the link across the Atlantic with the New World. Now, Japan's international position, in spite of its current crisis, and the general prospects for growth in the entire Asian continent (China and India being prime examples) mean that trade is being inexorably attracted towards the East, in a manner that has not occurred since the sixteenth century.

We therefore have to interpret this geo-economic transformation in the spirit of the Iberian and Italian navigators and traders of the early modern era who went in search of the 'route to the Indies'. It is no coincidence then that over the last decade, trade between Europe and Asia has grown at a higher rate than trade between the United States and Asia, exploding the myth that forecast a future in which Europe would be marginalized by the increasing importance of the Pacific.

(4) The signs of the Mediterranean's reawakening, at least from an economic point of view, are already there for all to see. As so often in the past, these signs are most evident in the dynamic trading activity of its ports. Algeciras, Valencia, Barcelona, Genoa, Naples, the newly created port of Gioia Tauro, Damietta, Ashdod, Haifa, Piraeus and many other centres along the shores of the Mediterranean, are all flourishing again as investments flow in and reorganization gets under way at one of the highest rates in the world. These are areas that not long ago were considered to be suffering stagnation and decline, undergoing restructuring, or simply becoming peripheral to the great trends in world development. These are profoundly important indicators whose significance is much greater than it would appear at first sight. They are signs of an immense shift in relations, and not just in the Mediterranean.

Because of the geo-economic and geopolitical events of the last thirty years, we have become too accustomed to seeing the Mediterranean in terms of oil trade, military manoeuvres and little else. But what is in fact emerging and will determine our future is a veritable explosion in global economic relations between Europe and Asia, especially the Far East. These relations have been followed through by a radical transformation of logistical systems. The new generation of container ships is now reaching us through the Suez Canal, which is increasingly the great artery that joins us to Asia. Not since the discovery of the Americas has the Mediterranean been as important as it is today and will be tomorrow. We must do our utmost to ensure that, as we establish the European Union, this objective importance is taken into account in our plans and increasingly becomes an integral part of European unity in the economic, political and social fields. I hope that within a generation we will be obliged to close that historical chapter so beloved of primary-school textbooks. This is the assertion that the discovery of America initiated the progressive and irreversible decline of the Mediterranean, which had been marginalized by the great trade routes that crossed the oceans to northern Europe. Ten years ago, three-quarters of European continental maritime traffic originated in northern ports and only a quarter in the Mediterranean. In those ten years, the ratio has been reduced to two-thirds against a third: a massive change for such a brief period. The change was due to Asia's continual growth, which in spite of its recent crisis continues to have increasing importance on the world stage.

(5) This new economic axis that points to the East can only increase the significance of the Mediterranean, which is the principal maritime junction for Eastern trade, because of the Suez Canal. These changes are compounded by those arising from the end of the cold war.

The difficult peace process in the Middle East might ultimately stabilize a region that has not yet been able to enjoy the same rates of growth as other areas of the world. The independence of the countries of central Asia also represents a great opportunity for the development of an area rich in natural resources. These processes have helped enlarge and strengthen the area around the Mediterranean basin, creating the right conditions for attracting capital and investments.

The imperatives of the global economy mean that as Europeans we cannot ignore the southern shore of the Mediterranean. The two other great advanced and industrialized areas of the world, North America and the Far East, have reserves of manpower close by and developing markets that offer very high returns on their capital. I am referring here to NAFTA,[1] which is moving towards enlargement in Latin America, and the Asian area of development which now even includes China. The southern Mediterranean enjoys both concentrations of technology and capital, and vast reserves of manpower, so it is the principal direction in which Europe can move to establish an area of development. The enlargement of the European Union to include eastern European countries is also an important step in this direction, although that region on its own does not have the critical mass, in the order of hundreds of millions of workers and consumers, that could be found in a Euro-Mediterranean economic zone.

It is therefore fundamental that Europe concentrates its efforts on the creation of a *great free trade area* that covers the majority of the Mediterranean countries. Otherwise, we run the risk of growing protectionist trends in the Old Continent in response to American and Asian competitors steeled by their contact with developing economies. The 'regional free-trade areas' are in fact an extremely positive factor, if they represent an intermediate stage on the road to genuine liberalization in the context of the World Trade Organization. But they could impede economic development, if perceived as regional 'fortresses' that attempt to defend themselves against a global competition they feel is unjust.

(6) The other fundamental reason for investing in the Mediterranean is of a political nature. We cannot ignore the fact that the greatest dangers to European civilization, in terms of migration, environmental devastation and terrorism, could come from the southern shore of the Mediterranean. We cannot shirk our duty to implement a careful and sensible policy to stabilize the area. Through the appropriate economic and political incentives, such a policy would have to help resolve international

and internal conflicts in those countries where fundamentalism threatens the fragile process of democratization. The events in Kuwait, as well as those in Palestine, Israel and Algeria, remind us that the international stability achieved after the fall of the Berlin Wall is a precious and fragile asset that we cannot take for granted.

In its planning documents, the European Commission has outlined a framework for the twelve countries in the southern and eastern Mediterranean, from Morocco to Turkey. Its forecast shows that, following a demographic explosion, the population of these countries will equal that of the European Union by 2025. The Commission also emphasizes the increasing gap in per capita income between them and the Union, and the low level of imports into the European Community from these countries. These factors are expected to result in increasing pressure for emigration to Europe, further chaotic concentrations of population in large urban areas, and a clear difference in the potential for development between African coastal countries and the coastal countries of the Middle East. Other critical factors are the backwardness of transport infrastructures, the incipient deficit in energy resources and pollution of the waters of the Mediterranean. The conclusion is that we need a policy of co-operation on economic and democratic development based on access for these countries to the Single European Maket, assistance with investments and training human resources, encouragement in the building of networks between enterprises, universities, public bodies and local authorities, and plans for containing pollution. It is a framework that has been objectively assessed, but its realization is not a foregone conclusion. It requires our commitment as a Union, and not only from an economic point of view, as can be seen from our peace mission to Albania.

However, let us take a realistic and up-to-date look at the great era of civilization that radiated out from the Mediterranean to the rest of the world. If we consider the emerging role that globalization is assigning to the different regions of the world and in particular to the ancient *mare nostrum*, then we can contemplate the relaunch of the Mediterranean as a cultural entity and see its wider strategic potential. It is an historic opportunity with an economic, political and moral dimension that the European Union cannot let slip.

(7) It is clear that, with projects on this grand scale, only Europe as a whole has the necessary resources and sufficient authority for effective policy decisions. It is when we look at contemporary events from a historical perspective that we become particularly aware of the need for an ambitious project to build a new Europe. As the eminent academic of the Real Academia,[2] José Marías de Yanguas Messía, prophetically argued in 1949:

> Europe must act for its own profound purposes. It has suffered enough impoverishment and too much geographical mutilation for the surviving nations to afford the luxury of economic autarchy and political nationalism. A much wider boundary is inexorably imposing itself on the nation state with its isolationist outlook. In other words, the fundamental task that Europe faces and will have to decide upon by itself, essentially comes down to integration, as opposed to the fragmentation that prevailed three hundred years ago at the Treaty of Westphalia and accustomed us to international anarchy. It matters little whether the progress is rapid or not, as long as the intention is firm and continuity guaranteed. The undertaking is difficult because the nation states will have to sacrifice to the collective interest a part of what up until now has been under their exclusive sovereignty.[3]

(8) We have already mentioned the need to proceed with greater integration of the European Union's institutions and policies. Our commitment and our daily activities are working in this direction. Having successfully dealt with the great challenge of monetary union, we now need to pursue with determination the review of our institutions, which was left unfinished in Amsterdam. Not only do we owe it to ourselves, but it is being demanded by the countries that are seeking to participate in planning the new Europe. Enlargement represents an extraordinary opportunity to play an active part in a historical process marked by progressive regional integration. In Europe, this phenomenon is not confined to a search for complementary markets and the creation of free-trade areas in order to optimize trading agreements. The future entry of new member states is taking on a powerful political significance and becoming a question of principle.

By defining a framework for entry negotiations with the countries of central and eastern Europe and the Mediterranean,[4] we have started to implement a process originally conceived by the European Charter at the close of the last decade. The mission to enlarge its frontiers is, in any case, written into the European Union's genetic code. So it is only natural to welcome countries that, following an enforced separation, wish to rejoin a shared tradition of culture, political commitment and economic development. The framework for entry negotiations with individual countries was therefore formulated with a great sense of responsibility. We evaluated full compliance with the criteria relating to the European Union's common system of political values and compatibility with the economies of the member states within a wide-ranging perspective. Each candidate has been able to put its cards on the table, in the knowledge that membership can act as a catalyst for development.

As Europe's borders move eastwards, we must not let this shift the balance away from the centre of gravity fundamentally defined by the Mediterranean. We therefore have to preserve and strengthen our historical, economic and cultural links with the southern shore of the Mediterranean. This political undertaking needs an appropriate institutional framework. This need was met by the Euro-Mediterranean Partnership, which was launched in 1995.[5] This has been an extremely important instrument for demonstrating Europe's concern for the other shore of 'our sea'. Only political and economic integration can strengthen the contacts between civilizations that we have shared for centuries. The Partnership should therefore not be seen as a network of agreements that have already resulted in the association of individual countries with the European Union, but rather as a training ground for new and more ambitious relations. On the other hand, this exercise cannot be divorced from Europe's commitment to the consolidation of the peace process in the Middle East. Participation in the Partnership by all the countries in the region confirms the initiative's profound political significance and encourages us to pursue our efforts in the current delicate stage of the peace process.

We should remember that the wider concept of security and the interdependencies that increasingly integrate our countries into the various geographical areas are forcing us to look at what is happening around us with renewed interest. The Mediterranean is a focal point of great changes that produce shock waves and generate new tensions of a political, economic and religious nature. Only a solid link between the two sides of the sea can guarantee a prospect of stability and at the same time avoid the sorry sight of men and women being forced by poverty and fear to abandon their homelands.

Notes

1 NAFTA, the North America Free Trade Agreement, was signed in 1993 by the United States, Canada and Mexico, and created a free-trade area in the continent.

2 I am referring here to the Real Academia de Ciencias Morales y Políticas in Madrid.

3 Cf. *Académicos vistos por académicos – Iuristas y Filósofos – José M. de Yanguas Messía* (Madrid: Real Academia de Ciencias Morales y Políticas, 1997), pp. 191–229.

4 I am again referring to the decisions taken by the European Summit held in Luxembourg in December 1997 and explained in chapters 1, 2 and 3. To date, as we know, there are five countries in central and eastern Europe with which the European Union has formally opened negotiations over membership, namely Estonia, Poland, the Czech Republic, Slovenia and Hungary, and in the Mediterranean there is Cyprus.

5 The Barcelona Conference in November 1995 marked the moment when Europe relaunched its commitment to the Mediterranean. A partnership was organized between the EU and non-EU Mediterranean with a strong political dimension as well as a series of economic and cultural initiatives. The prospect of creating a free-trade area by 2010 was also discussed. All the countries on the Mediterranean's southern and eastern shores except Libya took part in the exercise, with the addition of Malta and Cyprus. Provisions were made for entering into bilateral association agreements, and four have already been signed: Israel and Tunisia (1995), Morocco (1996) and Jordan (1997). In 1997, a preliminary accord was signed with the Palestinian National Authority. The question of the Euro-Mediterranean Partnership will be taken up again in the following chapter.

6

The single currency, technological competition and the Mediterranean's new role

(1) Fifty years ago, it was the intention of Europe's founding fathers to build peace between the peoples of Europe after centuries of war. Yet what they created was the greatest and most brilliant economic institution of our time. Tommaso Padoa-Schioppa has rightly pointed out that right from the beginning 'the aim of the European project was primarily *economic*. But its nature, its significance and its driving force were *political*, and the intention was to transform power, security, institutions and nation states.'[1] If we stop to consider for a moment the last stage in this extraordinary process, Economic and Monetary Union (EMU), we find further confirmation of this productive interaction between politics and economics. As a result of EMU, eleven nation states have voluntarily renounced their monetary sovereignty. An event of this magnitude has never previously occurred in history.[2] At the dawn of the twenty-first century, a country's currency, rather than its military strength, is the genuine symbol of its sovereignty. Giving it up is primarily a political decision.

Three Mediterranean countries, Spain, Portugal and Italy, have taken part in EMU, and Greece is rapidly approaching the macroeconomic convergence required by the Maastricht Treaty. This serves to emphasize a second point: that United Europe is already here and continues to develop through the joint efforts of the two great founding cultures, one Latin and one German. The progressive enlargement means that, after the Anglo-Saxon, the Slav culture will soon be added, as a result of the shift in the Union's borders to the east. We know very well, precisely because of all that has been achieved over these fifty years, that the diversity of European identities and cultures enriches Europe.

(2) In truth, the strength and credibility of a currency do not only express economic values. The euro is political Europe's visiting card. This is why I am convinced that we must now concentrate on two essential aspects of the integration process, by which I mean foreign policy and defence. In both these fields, we can now report some encouraging signals: the Amsterdam Treaty and the rationalization of the European defence industry as a condition for making the Common Foreign and Security Policy effective, although considerable reforms and other measures still have to be implemented. The effectiveness of foreign policy presupposes shared objectives and real solidarity between partners. Events in the Balkans do not only affect member states that are geographically close: the credibility of the whole of Europe is at stake. This is equally true of the immigration question. The great significance of the Schengen Agreement does not lie in the abolition of border controls between the member states. The real qualitative change is that these countries now share a common external border.

(3) This brief outline is sufficient to demonstrate what an extraordinary period of change Europe is still living through. Robert Schuman's 'declaration' in 1950 has gone down in history. When he piloted through the establishment of the European Coal and Steel Community, he made a statement that is still valid today: 'Europe cannot be made in a single moment or as a fully worked-out structure, but only through concrete achievements that create genuine solidarity.' It has undoubtedly been a long journey stretching from the pooling of coal and steel resources right through to today's single currency and on to closer political union in the near future, and it has been full of social and economic advances. We have created new supranational institutions that are capable of guiding the

behaviour of individual states, particularly in the management
of their economies. Democracy and the free market have been
considerably expanded to embrace the greater part of the Old
Continent.

In order to clarify our ideas, let us stop to consider the
structure of this veritable economic giant, which is destined to
play an extremely significant role on the world stage, before
we go on to look more closely at its southern shore and the
area that faces onto the Mediterranean.

(4) Whether you consider the European Union in its entirety
or only examine the euro zone (so-called Euroland), some
essential economic facts appear particularly significant. I refer
to the magnitude of wealth produced, macro- and microeconomic policies and the structure of European industry. Here I
will limit myself to summarizing them briefly.

(a) *The magnitude of the European economy*. I have already
    stated that in 1997, Euroland's total GDP came to about
    80 per cent of the GDP for the United States. Clearly
    the GDP for all of the fifteen member states is quantitat-
    ively higher than that of the United States. Euroland is
    also a trading power, and its share of world exports to
    countries outside Euroland is higher than that of the
    United States.[3]
(b) *Macroeconomic convergence and microeconomic reforms*.
    Leaving aside the statistics for the moment, the process
    of macroeconomic convergence laid down by the five
    parameters of the Maastricht Treaty led to a culture of
    stability. It has established a solid basis for commencing
    the next cycle of development of the European economy.
    The cost of money in Italy is at its lowest level since the
    seventies, which were the golden years for our economy.
    The same could be said of many other countries. Invest-
    ment, particularly in private enterprise, will benefit from
    lower interest rates and from having inflation under control,
    and investment has always been the essential ingredient
    for economic growth. The great problem that Europe is
    facing today is insufficient growth combined with a high
    level of unemployment, especially among the young.

We can be absolutely certain that we are living through a delicate moment of transition between a number of achievements (the attainment of macroeconomic stability, which is guaranteed by the Stability and Growth Pact) and the full working through of its positive effects (the creation of new jobs). If the appropriate microeconomic reforms continue, we will be able to gather their fruits. Microeconomic reforms will definitely have to include increased flexibility in the labour market and a reduction in the tax burden that affects the cost of labour. But it does not end here. A *policy mix* consistent with recovery and growth in Europe must involve a major effort to train the workforce (I am thinking here of technological training) and research and development activity (R&D).

This is suggested by an examination of the structure of European industry, which is still too focused on tradi-tional production, while leadership in high-tech products (everything including microelectronics and information technologies) is firmly in the hands of the United States. Let us give this our consideration.

(c) *The structure of European industry.* The economic devel-opments of the last quarter of a century, commonly called globalization, demonstrate that enterprises in countries that have been industrialized for a long time cannot compete with developing countries in production with a low technological content, namely production in which unskilled labour prevails. We cannot escape the fact that European industry needs to specialize in production with a high technological content and a high 'added value', where high skill levels are required of all the workforce and where there is a high input from scientific and tech-nological research.

An example could assist us to understand better what is at stake. Of the current twenty-five largest American companies, nineteen either did not exist or were tiny before 1960. The best-known examples are Microsoft and Intel, neither of which existed at that time. Conversely, an examination of the twenty-five largest European com-panies shows that none of them is new, as they have all existed for over thirty years. One of this century's great economists, Joseph A. Schumpeter, would have applied his celebrated definition of 'creative destruction' to the American situation: new industries, created out of technical and scientific progress, replace the old ones, which in the meantime have become obsolete.

I believe that this lesson is worth pointing out. Europe must learn to turn its considerable scientific and technological knowledge into business opportunities. Several things would be required, starting with a more modern financial system in which venture capital fulfils its proper role. All observers correctly stress the importance of the role of merchant banks and providers of risk capital in the development of American high-tech companies. However, we should not forget that Europe is no longer putting enough effort into teaching theoretical and applied sciences for our continent to play its proper part in the future of our planet. European technology has not grown to the same extent as its affluence and its labour costs. The risk of being crushed between the United States and the new players in the world economy is still very great, even at a time of great crisis in Asia.

(4) While referring the reader back to the previous chapters for a study in greater depth of the typical features of the economy of the European Union and the euro zone in particular, I would like to reaffirm that European integration has been a genuine success story. It has benefited every country that has joined during one of its different waves of entry. From the moment of joining, each member state has found itself operating in a *wider and more competitive market*, where the barriers to the free circulation of goods, services and capital gradually decreased following the Treaty of Rome in 1957 to the point where they disappeared.

The increased size of the domestic market, with the subsequent possibility of companies achieving greater economies of scale, constituted a powerful factor in growth. Tommaso Padoa-Schioppa wrote that:

> During the first thirty years after the War, Europe caught up in many ways with other areas of the world that were then more

developed. If you compare Italy's per capita income with that
of Switzerland, the richest European country outside the Community, you will find that it rose from 38 per cent then to 77 per
cent in 1992.[4]

Of course, Italy's performance is particularly significant, given
that it was linked to the European adventure right from the
beginning. However, close examination shows that European
integration has given all the countries that have joined considerable benefits in terms of cohesion. A recent study by the
London School of Economics has thrown light on this extraordinary process.[5] This study states that:

> for over four decades, there has been a considerable reduction
> in the gap in development between the EU's central and peri-
> pheral regions, which means that the Community's integration,
> first of an economic and then of a political nature, produced
> the convergence of its regional economies between 1950 and
> 1995. This has been confirmed by the study of 80 regional
> cases for the period between 1970 and 1995, using variable per
> capita GDPs in ecus and PPPs (purchasing power parities) and
> by the study of 74 regional cases for the period 1950–70.

(5) Four decades of convergence, integration and cohesion have
meant that the Europe of the 1950s (a Europe that had its
centre of development shifted towards the north) has been
replaced by a more cohesive Europe that has concentrated an
enormous potential for growth in its *Mediterranean regions*, the
Iberian peninsula and above all Italy.

The Mediterranean has always been a single system and a
meeting place for diverse cultures and peoples. In spite of the
great economic, institutional, political and religious differences
that the twentieth century produced between the countries facing each other across 'our sea', the new century has opened with
more than a few hopeful signs of renewed dialogue between
Europe and the Mediterranean.

When speaking of what the Mediterranean could be in the
twenty-first century, it is worth remembering that in November 1995 we held the first Euro-Mediterranean Conference in
Barcelona and it concluded with a formal declaration. The fundamental idea in the Barcelona Declaration was that of creating

throughout this geographical area 'a zone of dialogue, trade and co-operation that guarantees peace, stability and prosperity'. The Barcelona Conference not only provided for the creation of a free-trade area in the Mediterranean before 2010 (which would mean the involvement of 30–40 countries with a population of 600–800 million people), but also initiated a political and strategic dialogue. This is probably the only way to create growth in the southern countries, which will learn useful lessons by 'importing' our *community institutions*.

Europe can certainly boast four decades of convergence, integration and cohesion. It can certainly boast an enhanced role for its Mediterranean countries. However, these phenomena have not been a simple and automatic historical process in the past and they will not be one in the future. Immense strategic capability is needed if we are to carry through these interwoven historical developments and exploit their full potential. It would be worth briefly running over what has been achieved so far.

(6) In the post-war decades, the Mediterranean regions on the European side looked to the heart of Europe beyond the Pyrenees and the Alps, for fear of slipping back into the Mediterranean. Some have argued that at that time, this area was 'synonymous with a shift to the Third World and authoritarianism',[6] as opposed to economic and democratic development in mid- and northern European countries that were engaged in the process of western integration. The financial centre (as defined in recent European Union documents), which is a macro-region covering London, Paris and now also Berlin, together with the central Franco-German area, constituted the economic foundations on which integration was built.

The material effects of this geo-economic and geopolitical gravitation can be seen from the fact that development potential decreases as you gradually move away from these areas, in spite of the considerable reduction in differences that I referred to earlier. This potential is measured not only in terms of income, but also in terms of the ability to control international economic relations in peripheral areas of the European Community and particularly in Mediterranean areas. The situation changes substantially as European economic integration gradually strengthens, and the European Community becomes a complex whole, and is no longer simply a heterogeneous group of states that are medium-sized from an economic and political point of view. This 'surplus' potential arising from integration has been put to the test by the crisis and transformation of eastern Europe and the Balkans, on which the Community has, to date, prioritized its efforts.

Also as a result of the formation of an integrated market and economic structure in Europe, a second factor of enormous strategic importance has been the building of closer relations between the European Community and the emerging economic powers in the Far East. These stronger ties have been progressively offsetting the previous explosion of trade across the Pacific (between the Far East and the United States). This second great source of strength (a further expression of the surplus potential arising from European integration) has strongly affected maritime trade in the Mediterranean. As we have seen, Mediterranean ports (Barcelona, Algeciras and Valencia in Spain, and Genoa, La Spezia and Gioia Tauro in Italy) have become major international termini, after having been marginalized for a long period in relation to the North Sea ports.

The European Community will probably not evolve in the direction of a relatively closed macro-region structured internally around a core area and supplemented by economic peripheries. It now looks more likely that it will evolve in the direction of an area of great complexity and internal variety, whose potential as a community is projected outside into a number of regional areas of activity. In this sense, the Mediterranean area of activity takes on a strategic importance in the world, and over the medium term, it could at last recover the historic role that made it the cradle of the first world civilization. This role, I repeat, is not automatic and requires a further internal development of the European Community. The creation of a single currency, combined with a limited mobility of production factors, might in fact reverse the past tendency to reduce the gap between central and peripheral regions. There is therefore a risk that the strong part of the system increasingly attracts the business brains and the decision-making bodies. The growing number of agreements between larger companies, the increase in corporate mergers, and the concentration of financial markets as a result of the euro will produce a growing challenge to the peripheral countries. We must be aware of this, and be ready to meet these challenges by working to a greater extent on training human resources and building forms of co-operation between Mediterranean countries that we have too often ignored. This would make us less dependent on the 'strong' regions of Europe.

(7) Today the Mediterranean poses enormous political problems concerning security and the coexistence of politically hetero-geneous regimes, and economic problems of interdependence. At the political level, we should not in any way underestimate the steps taken by Europe to resolve the Albanian conflict. On this occasion, European and, in particular, Mediterranean countries (such as Spain, Portugal, France and Italy) responded decisively, and a crisis in the troubled region of the former Yugoslavia was kept under control. This mission, although of a relatively modest size, has been the sole example of a peace-keeping initiative undertaken and completed by a group of Euro-pean countries, without the need for American involvement.

It should also be stressed that the development of relations with the Maghrib countries of the western Mediterranean was left too late. Indeed, relations with these countries are still marked by the not so distant colonial past that still leads to a bilateral approach. These relations are also complicated by pressures of emigration from these countries to Mediterranean areas of Europe. The entire European Community therefore has to approach the question not simply in terms of commer-cial interests. We must promote regional economic integration between the two shores of the western Mediterranean, with Spain, Italy and France in the front line and acting as spokes-men for the Union. The first signs of this integration can be traced back to the relocation of manufacturing production from the centre to the Maghrib region by a certain number of Euro-pean companies, and its development of European tourism, as well as its more traditional role in supplying Europe with raw materials and agricultural produce.

Clearly, in an era of globalization, these 'regional' relations must be supported by a wider perspective of mutual interests. This is where the Mediterranean's decisive strategic role on the world stage comes into play. As far as Mediterranean relations are concerned, we must ultimately be able, as the European Union, to hold together and develop three great strengths. First, we have the economic potential, political prestige and sense of responsibility that arise from the fact that we are now a supranational entity with an extraordinary cultural heritage. Second, we have the potential for regional economic integration, which arises from the different levels of development, the differentials in production costs and the still significant traces of a long history of cultural symbiosis. Third, Europe and North Africa share an interest in developing the Mediterranean's role as a centre for intercontinental trade, which is growing fast in this 'global' era.

(8) We now have to put more effort into the Euro-Mediterranean Partnership. The European Union in recent years has been devoting its energies to the two fundamental and necessary objectives of EMU and enlargement to the east. Today, we must turn our attention to this new frontier of development and co-operation. This is true for the EU as a whole and for countries like Spain and Italy, that border the Mediterranean. *Italy between Europe and the Mediterranean: a Choice That No Longer Has To Be Made* is the title of a book recently published in Italy.[7] In it Nino Andreatta points out that the title is 'important for the freedom it brings'.[8] We are no longer obliged to make this choice, and we no longer have to look to the north rather than the south. The headlong development of Asia has helped restore to the Mediterranean its ancient centrality. I have on many occasions expressed my personal conviction that we are facing the most important geopolitical shift since the discovery of America in distant 1492.

Notes

1 T. Padoa-Schioppa, 'Che cosa ci ha insegnato l'avventura europea', *Il Mulino*, 6 (1998).
2 The few previous historical examples of monetary union were, as I pointed out in ch. 1, much more modest both in terms of the economic strength of the countries involved and the institutional framework (management of monetary policy, money in circulation, etc.).

3   A comparative study at macroeconomic level (GDP, international trade, etc.) between the United States and Euroland (i.e. the group of countries that took part in the launch of the euro on 1 January 1999) was carried out in ch. 4. For the relevant figures, see in particular nn. 3 and 4.
4   Padoa-Schioppa, 'Che cosa ci ha insegnato l'avventura europea'.
5   R. Leonardi, *Convergence, Cohesion and Integration in the European Union* (London: Macmillan, 1995), see esp. ch. 5.
6   S. Silvestri in his introduction to N. Andreatta et al., *L'Italia tra Europa e Mediterraneo: il bivio che non c'è più* (Bologna: Il Mulino–Collana Arel, 1998), pp. 8–12.
7   Andreatta et al., *L'Italia tra Europa e Mediterraneo*.
8   Ibid., pp. 15–19.

Part III

Europe on the
World Stage

7

Europe and Asia at the turn of the century

(1) Relations between Europe and Asia are now more important than they have been for decades, because Europe was previously preoccupied with other problems and uncertainties within its own region. On an economic level, the process of European integration had to be carried through, and it was not at all clear whether Europe would become a free-trade area or a protectionist block. This economic uncertainty produced alternating periods of 'Euro-phoria' and 'Euro-sclerosis'. On a political level, our major concern was the division of our continent as a result of the cold war. Now, at the start of a new century, these problems have finally been overcome.

In economic terms, the European Union has successfully prepared for monetary union and, at the same time, it is confident of its role in a free-trade system that it helped consolidate during the Uruguay Round of negotiations. Politically, the end of the cold war allowed us to launch the process of enlargement that emerged from the Luxembourg European Council in December 1997. Although this difficult task will initially absorb a large part of the Union's resources, the final result will be a larger and more self-confident Union, able to project its influence well beyond its continental borders. As the European Union's share of the world economy grows and the political problems caused by the continent's division begin to fade, Europe will be able to devote its attention to wider issues.

(2) Thus Europe is about to conclude the ambitious project that was started four decades ago by our founding fathers. The great vision shown by Monnet, Schuman, Adenauer and De Gasperi had three fundamental features. First, by putting our centuries-long political conflict in the past, we would be able to channel greater resources to more fruitful objectives. Second, the establishment of a large single market would lead to the economies of scale needed to compete in the world economy. Third, Europe would provide a common framework for the national political systems and force them to become modern industrial democracies.

Since the establishment of the European Community, progress in these directions has influenced international relations beyond the Community's borders, through the active participation of its member states in the global institutional network and, above all, by setting a powerful example. This is why Italy, one of the larger countries in the Union, enthusiastically supported the European project right from the beginning. More recently, it is why the government I had the honour to lead made Europe one of its major priorities.

It is precisely because European Monetary Union is now an established fact, that the European project cannot restrict itself to European affairs and must adopt a wider perspective. From a monetary perspective, the creation of the euro and its success as a new reserve currency on a par with the dollar implies revolutionary transformations. It will give rise to a more complex international monetary system no longer based on a single currency. At the same time, it will be more stable, because the financial situation will no longer depend on development within a single economy, but on a varied set of strong and stable currencies. I therefore believe that the euro will herald great opportunities and exercise a beneficial effect on the world economy, although it will require careful orchestration and diplomacy to manage the transition from one system to the other.

(3) These changes can no longer be ignored, given their relevance to politics and the global economy. European integration, Asian expansion (although weakened by its recent crisis, its underlying dynamic remains intact) and the dense network of relations between 'open' economies have created a genuinely

global market, in which Europe and Asia are no longer isolated partners but part of a wider system.

The particular nature of these economic processes, which are driven more by *direct investments* from foreign sources than by *traditional trading relations*, has increased each country's interest in the economies of the others. Modern companies do not perceive distant countries solely as potential markets for their goods, but also as opportunities for investment and the transfer of production. This means that increasing liberalization is almost irreversible, because companies whose assets are located in various countries would oppose any attempts at protectionism. Consequently, the economy of each country has a much greater interest in the good performance of the other economies, because investments abroad and inward investments from abroad increasingly contribute to a country's wealth.[1]

Europe has realized that it can no longer afford to ignore an important part of the world that includes great nations like India, China and Japan, and will soon be the largest economic region in the world.[2] Europe will be unable to formulate a truly global policy until it manages to be a player on the Asian stage. Trade between Europe and Asia has increased by more than 100 per cent since 1988 – more rapidly than trade between the United States and Asia. This was no accident and was partly the result of the institutional policy developed at the ASEM Summit (Asia–Europe Meeting) held in Bangkok in March 1996 (the second ASEM Summit was held in London in April 1998).

We have reopened another great trade route between Europe and Asia. The increasingly substantial trade and flows of capital are as important for today's economy as the Silk Road was in the sixteenth century. This gives the lie to those who forecast a 'peaceful century', in which Europe will have a marginal role. This is why I do not agree with the pessimists who expect a geo-economic conflict between autonomous continental units, which, according to Lester Thurow, will clash head-on. Naturally, the world economy will continue to be marked by competition, but governments will increasingly do all they can to give companies in their countries access to foreign markets and to encourage foreign investors at home, rather than withdrawing from the world economy and weakening the ability of their national companies to compete.

(4) These positive developments have been overshadowed by the pessimism that resulted from the crisis in the Far East in the autumn of 1997, which caused lower growth in the region and lower levels of trade with other regions. I do not believe, however, that the problem is of a structural nature or that it will have any long-term repercussions on growth in Asia or other regions. I believe that this crisis is no different from any other, just as I always believed that the previous period of expansion was not in any intrinsic way exceptional. There is no 'Asian virus', just as there was never an 'Asian path to growth' based on culturally specific factors. Asia enjoyed strong economic expansion because it had all the requirements in terms of physical and human infrastructures, and not for any cultural reasons. Its economies will therefore continue to grow once they have overcome their current problems. Besides, it was unrealistic to expect that such rapid growth and the transformation of traditional societies into modern economies over the brief span of two decades would not produce tensions within the financial and regulatory systems of those countries. They had not had enough time to adjust to their new status. In any case, there is nothing stopping these countries from making these adjustments. This is why Italy and Europe as a whole support the International Monetary Fund by providing assistance and consultancy services to the countries hardest hit by the crisis, and I am sure that they will come out of it healthier than before.

(5) The major obstacles to progress in Asia are more political in nature. In this region, relations between neighbouring countries are often very tense, and concerns over security are such that the possibility of a disastrous military conflict cannot be ruled out. The development of economic relations can be useful, as it is a strong incentive to avoid political conflicts, but the solutions to these security problems can only be of a political nature.

The greatest risk concerns the future role of China, whose growth into a great power will have a genuinely international impact. The international community can deal with this development in two ways. It could attempt to contain and restrict China by constructing a network of local and global alliances around Peking. This, however, could prove to be a self-fulfilling prophecy, as it would alienate China and generate potentially uncontrollable regional tensions. The balance of power in Asia would be extremely delicate, given that the number of protagonists and the military technologies at their disposal would make it dangerous to engage in strategies based on deterrence. On the other hand, China could be accepted, involved in regional and world diplomacy and allowed to make a constructive contribution to international politics and the global economy, thus developing interests favourable to the maintenance of stability.

All the regional powers should join forces to establish a common definition of acceptable behaviour, in order to defuse and isolate potential sources of regional instability. This could mean moderating policies that are not acceptable to neighbouring countries. However, I believe that the economic and security benefits arising from international stability would be worth the effort.

(6) Thus the future promises a greater diplomatic role for Europe in Asia. This role depends not only on closer economic ties, but also on the experience acquired by Europe in building institutions. Productive forms of co-operation can be launched in a short period using existing institutions, such as the World Trade Organization or the United Nations, where questions of common interest can be debated. These can range from the liberalization of financial services to peacekeeping operations or nuclear proliferation. There could be co-operation in reforming the United Nations and its Security Council, where the number of seats should be increased to allow the participation of those countries that contribute most to its universal mandate in terms of financial, military and political support.[3]

(7) Only two hundred years ago, Asia was by far the richest region in the world, and its civilization was probably the most advanced. Spectacular growth over the last few years, in spite of the recent crisis, has resulted in a situation in which it would not be unrealistic to expect a return to that happy state of affairs. As I have said elsewhere in this book, I do not believe that there will be a 'clash of civilizations'. There are

opportunities to work together, as long as Asians and Europeans are ready to show commitment and goodwill to each other. New fault lines have not appeared to replace the old ones, following the end of the cold war and its rigid divisions. There has simply been a reaffirmation of the importance of diplomacy as a way of finding solutions to shared problems that sooner or later would hinder our progress towards a better future.

Notes

1   There is now an immense literature on globalization, as well as its causes and effects. If I had to choose one well-documented summary, it would be the eight articles in the 'Schools brief' published by *The Economist* between 18 October and 6 December 1997. The first of these articles presented some very interesting data for understanding the forces behind the increasing integration of national economies. In the period 1980–96, the average annual growth of international trade in real terms was twice the growth in GDP at world level (5% compared with about 2.5%). However, inward investments in turn grew much more rapidly than trade, with an average annual increase of 9%. Trading in foreign exchange and stock and bond securities increased at considerably higher rates (20–25%). See 'One world' ('Schools brief'), *The Economist*, 18 October 1997, pp. 103–4.

2   A projection to 2020 of the changes in the distribution of world production, worked out by OECD in Paris, is analysed in ch. 8.

3   In essence, the Italian proposal for the reform of the Security Council (submitted in 1994 and later continuously refined in concert with an extremely wide range of members of the United Nations) provides for an increase in non-permanent members of the Council itself, which would make the body more representative. This objective would not be achieved by simply extending the number of permanent members, as strongly advocated by other countries.

8

European industry and finance up against international competition

(1) In recent years we have been witnessing the end of a great historical cycle that started at the end of eighteenth century with the Industrial Revolution, a cycle that effectively subordinated the world economy to the Western one. For instance, the size of the European economy in relation to the world economy is now returning to the level it was at in 1750, after having passed through a period of absolute dominance that lasted two and a half centuries. This is not due to any failure on the part of the European economy, which – quite the contrary – appears to have been rejuvenated, but rather to a process of market globalization that has favoured the rapid development of emerging countries. This phenomenon was only temporarily interrupted by the recent crisis in Asia, and we can reasonably expect levels of development to draw markedly closer in the coming decades.

Economic and Monetary Union sets the seal on this transformation. It acknowledges the fact that Europe's national economies are no longer the reference points they once were. Today we need to build an economic zone with a 'critical mass' suited to the new international environment. There was a time when the majority of European companies compared themselves with their competitors in other European countries. Now comparisons have an increasingly global dimension, and European companies find themselves up against tough competition, particularly from America and Japan. Competition within Europe is no longer the sole driving force behind development, as in the past. Today, we have to operate on a much wider stage where competition takes on a truly global perspective. The ensuing push for rationalization and simplification in the world economy opens the way for untrammelled growth in competitive capitalism.

The creation of a great monetary area in Europe provides the European economies with those benefits of scale they need if they are to compete openly and hold their heads high in the international market. However, it is not a process that will lead Europe into a protectionist struggle with the other great economic zones in North America and eastern Asia. On the contrary, I believe that it will put European companies in a position to benefit fully from the lower tariff barriers ratified by the Uruguay Round and pursued by the World Trade Organization. The trading blocs will be building blocks rather than stumbling blocks on the road to global free trade.

(2) Even before its completion, the process of monetary unification has already produced substantial gains in the fight against inflation and in bolstering the international monetary system, after the instability of the seventies and early eighties had weakened the Western economies. As the experience of the gold standard and Bretton Woods has shown, monetary stability is a necessary prerequisite for lasting growth in the economy and trade. In periods of instability, such as during the two world wars or the oil crisis, the fragility of the international economy tragically resurfaces.

This does not mean, however, that European integration should be restricted to monetary questions. What we have to do is take a fresh look at the cultural and economic heritage of 'European capitalism' or, to be more precise, the different forms of capitalism that coexist in Europe. The great drive for Europe's progressive liberalization, which has brought great benefits through a substantial growth in exports, is in fact being achieved through the monetary union project. European companies will have to turn to a much larger market to boost their exports: a challenge that they are capable of meeting.

(3) Monetary unification will also add to the importance of social and structural reforms of capitalism in Europe. At a time

when monetary policy is no longer decided at national level, and even fiscal policy is restricted by the need to adjust national economies to the single currency, the only way the European market can grow and become competitive is through a profound reform of the operating environment. The state's role will therefore be 'leaner', but this does not mean that it will be any less important. Its task will be to ensure massive investments in human and intellectual capital. It will have to guarantee free competition on behalf of the consumer. It will need to create straightforward and innovative legal structures to encourage investment and favour those services essential for entrepreneurial development. It is now time to review one by one the questions that I raised in the introduction, starting with the launch of EMU.

(4) EMU, as I have pointed out several times, is an act of faith in Europe and a challenge within the wider context of the world economy. The birth of the euro is Europe's great contribution to international monetary stability. A new reserve currency now flanks the dollar. Both are based on economies of great substance, strength and tradition. I have frequently referred in this book to the very similar magnitude and trading power of these two giants of the world economy. Nevertheless, there are some significant differences between the two areas. The first is the different weight of foreign trade (there is a current account surplus on Euroland's balance of payments and a current account deficit in the case of the United States). The second is the public accounts situation (Europe has taken decisive action towards improving its situation, while the United States has already brought its public accounts back into credit). The third is the unemployment rate (in Europe it is more than double the rate in the United States) and the general conditions of the labour market.[1]

(5) The fundamental objective is therefore to get Europe back on the path of strong and prolonged economic growth. The legacy of recent years will be particularly valuable in this search for macroeconomic stability. By bringing public borrowing under control, the national governments have ceased to offload debt onto future generations. Anti-inflation measures and the

subsequent reduction in interest rates have created the conditions for a new investment cycle. Exchange-rate stability has generated business confidence and enhanced the value and effect of true competition between companies. Recent experience has shown that there is no time distinction between 'phase one' and 'phase two' in economic policy. The measures taken to balance budgets have created the right conditions in the whole of Europe for a recovery that is not purely short-term. At the same time, all member states have introduced measures to assist growth.

In the case of Italy, I am referring to the reform of the civil service, the tax system and the labour market, reorganization of the educational structure and reform of the rules of corporate governance.[2] Following the Maastricht Treaty, the Stability and Growth Pact (signed in Dublin in December 1996) moved further in this direction by imposing very stringent restrictions on the ability of member states to resort to borrowing, and therefore obliging all of them to adopt prudent structural policies.

I have already mentioned the general principle that informs the new Europe: 'Let's get Europe back to work.' Given that in the Europe of the single currency, there will be a single monetary policy, transferred to the supranational level, and there will also be restrictions on the use of expansionist fiscal policies as a result of controls on public finances, the role of microeconomic policies will be considerably strengthened. Such policies should stimulate private economic enterprise as liberalization gathers pace in the European and, more generally, the world economy.

(6) As I said at the beginning of this chapter, the world economy is experiencing a period of extraordinary change. In reality, the West is no longer the only important player on the world stage. Although the comparison between the European Union and the United States still remains valid, we also have to look elsewhere, particularly in the direction of Asia and Latin America.

A recent OECD study outlined two possible scenarios for world economic growth between now and 2020,[3] which it called 'high performance' (the best-case scenario) and 'business as usual' ('any old how', so-so). Leaving aside the quantitative predictions on which the two scenarios are based, the principal difference lies in their forecasts of how much progress member states are likely to make with structural reforms, such as liberalization of trade and investments, adjustments to taxation and reform of the labour market. Of the many future indicators, it would be worth considering the following.

(a) *There is currently a global convergence of income levels.*[4] In 1995, the United States still accounted for 20 per cent of the world's GDP (equal to 32 trillion dollars), Europe for 22 per cent and Japan for 8 per cent. In 2020, the 'pie' representing the world's wealth will, according to the more favourable scenario, be worth 106 trillion dollars, and the United States' share will have fallen to 11 per cent, Europe's to 12, and Japan's to 5, while 35 per cent will be accounted for by the so-called Big Five that are not OECD members (Russia, China including Hong Kong, Indonesia, India and Brazil). It should be remembered that, in 1995, these countries had 21 per cent of the world's GDP. I do not believe that this long-term scenario will be radically modified by the crisis that in very recent times has struck Indonesia and Brazil.

(b) *If we look more closely at the OECD countries, it is the growth in productivity in relation to the accumulation of capital and the increase in the workforce that is seen as the main determinant for growth in GDP over the long term.* This is not surprising, given the difference in demographic trends between Europe and the other regions in the world, and given the increasingly central role of technological progress in determining the wealth of nations. In the opinion of the OECD, there are four principal factors capable of strengthening growth in productivity: reforms to the regulatory system and legislation governing the stimulation of competition, accelerated liberalization of trade, faster technological progress and greater investment in human capital.

(c) *There is currently a profound shift in the composition of world production as a result of increasing international specialization.* The great distinction made by the OECD is between 'agriculture/food processing' and 'consumer goods' on the one hand, and 'skill-intensive capital goods' on the other. The share of world agricultural production in non-OECD countries will grow by more than half by 2020, keeping pace with the growth in domestic demand. In the case of consumer goods, the share of world production in the non-OECD countries will depend on export growth, which in turn will make it possible to fund the increasing imports of capital goods. Consequently, the production of capital goods requiring skill-intensive labour will acquire central importance in the OECD countries. In 2020, the OECD countries will be responsible for two-thirds of the world production of capital goods. This data should be complemented by an understanding of the increasing importance of services in generating wealth: in 2020, services will account for over 70 per cent in the OECD countries and about 60 per cent in the other countries.

(7) Naturally, the competition between the more industrialized countries of the world and the developing ones is the first level for consideration. A second level is the competition within the OECD countries, particularly between the European Union, the United States and Japan: the so-called Triad. This is the aspect that we should now turn to. There is a vast corpus of socio-economic literature, mainly dating from the early nineties, that examines the competition between these three different areas of economic development, and highlights the different performance in terms of economic growth and social cohesion. In chapter 1, I described at length the welfare model that western European countries have built in recent decades. On the one hand, I emphasized the role it has played and continues to play in fostering cohesion – which ultimately also means greater economic growth. On the other hand, I highlighted the reforms required by this welfare model of ours.

We need to achieve a twin 'compatibility'. The first is eminently macroeconomic (the restrictions imposed on the deficit and government borrowing mean that we have to bring social expenditure back within the bounds of sustainable growth). The second compatibility concerns the new social dynamics and the labour market in particular: with the growing need for a highly skilled workforce and the increasing mobility demanded by young people, we need stronger collective institutions devoted to youth training and the retraining of employees.

When Michel Albert, Ralf Dahrendorf, Ronald Dore and Lester Thurow,[5] to mention just a few of the more authoritative academics, put the debate on the 'dynamic of capitalist models' at the top of the agenda, what they were concerned with was this wider approach to industrialized societies. This approach sees each particular model of capitalism not only for its 'productive' features, but goes further to encompass more specifically social features and aspects more closely linked to civil society.

(8) In stressing this wider approach to models of capitalism, we must not however lose sight of the fact that the economic strength of one model in relation to another rests primarily on its industrial and financial systems. The most striking feature of the American model is an extraordinary capacity to create new jobs and new high-tech companies. Conversely, the worrying aspect of Europe is its high level of unemployment, particularly among the young.

This does not cover all the differences between the performance of the United States and that of the European Union, which are naturally many-sided. The example does, however, give an idea of where we should be going and what target we should be aiming at. I continue to believe that putting the talents of our young people to good use is the most important objective of all.

(9) In the second half of the 1990s, a group of authoritative economists at the MIT, under the direction of Robert Solow, carried out a research project which was published with the evocative title of *Made in America – Regaining the Productive Edge*.[6] In the mid-1980s, America found itself in a situation in which the 'paper economy' was triumphant. Manufacturing industry was losing its traditional centrality and its technological superiority. In the same period, Japan was setting itself up as an economic and industrial power of world importance, and the European Community was launching its Single Market programme, which was to produce so many positive results.

Ten years later, the world economic situation appears very different, even if you only consider the Triad. The United States has regained its technological leadership. There is a crisis in Japan (and in South-East Asia in general). The European economy is displaying both strengths and weaknesses. Not unsurprisingly, a report published under the auspices of the European Commission is entitled *Made in Europe*.[7] Robert Solow writes in the introduction: 'Europe in 1998 is not America in 1989', because there were many developments in production systems over these ten years. Over the entire period there was an increasing interconnection between manufacturing and production services, and a greater use by companies of outsourcing strategies that went beyond national borders to take advantage of production sites with low labour costs. Although it is true that this historical and economic parallel should be treated with caution, Solow's opinion is irrefutable when he states that 'companies in the advanced countries cannot compete with poorer countries in production areas dominated by unskilled labour'. This is why it is so necessary in Europe, one of the three most advanced areas of the world, to specialize in industries with an intense research input and a high technological content. In short, such forms of production would require skills from the entire workforce.

(10) In this context, we could ask ourselves: where does European industry fit in today? In which sectors does it demonstrate technological excellence, and in which does it suffer from American or Japanese supremacy? In the following analysis I will outline a brief picture of the structure of European industry, and then move on to some of the proposals for economic policy in the wider context of a Europe with a single currency (a powerful factor for attracting international financial investment) and a stable macroeconomic framework (the Maastricht 'dividend').

The most significant features of the way European industry is structured have to do with *export specialization sectors*, where there is a dynamic network of SMEs [translator's note: small and medium-sized enterprises] that are typical of all European countries, and with large corporations. We can start by stating that SMEs form the backbone of the 16 million enterprises in the EU,[8] more than 90 per cent of which employ less than 10 people, and very many are one-person businesses. One truly distinctive feature is that they are often organized in 'business parks' where the economies of scale are achieved as a system rather than as a single enterprise. SMEs operate in practically all business sectors, although the so-called 'fashion' industries (clothing, footwear, etc.) and instrumental mechanics are their preferred fields of activity. It is possible in these industries to split up the manufacturing cycle between several enterprises, creating the conditions for a business park. Recent international summits at G7, G8 and European level devoted unprecedented attention to SMEs and business parks, which constitute a veritable social innovation. We can say with pride that the business parks of Italy represent an Italy where not only is industry efficient and the labour market close to full employment, but where there is also social cohesion.

Returning to the structure of European industry, a second important feature concerns the largest enterprises. The emphasis on SMEs should not overshadow their number and importance in certain industrial sectors. If we take the top 200 industrial groups in the world as they were in the mid-1990s,[9] 69 were European, 64 American, 53 Japanese and 14 from other countries. The Europeans achieved excellent performances in the chemical, pharmaceutical, food and oil-refining sectors. American and Japanese groups dominated electronics and information technology. Lastly, there was shared leadership of what has been called the 'industry of all industries': General Motors, Ford, Toyota and Daimler-Benz took the top positions in the list of car manufacturers.

Moving on from our specializations and strengths to look at the weaknesses in our European industrial system, the major consideration concerns its insufficient innovativeness, especially when compared with American industry. I have already referred to Europe's poor performance compared with America when it comes to the creation of new successful enterprises in the high-tech sectors. It will be remembered that Microsoft and Intel are examples of excellence. We have come to the 'European paradox', and on this point we conclude our examination of industrial specialization. Why is there this European paradox? Is it perhaps because Europe cannot boast a single world leader in the fundamental industries of microelectronics and information technology, and continues to dominate the world stage in the old industrial sectors, such as chemicals? Of course, this is a weakness in relation to the United States and the other great world economic power, Japan, but the paradox also arises from a more general consideration. Most indicators of scientific and technological 'production' (I refer here to the number of patents, scientific publications of international importance, and so on) show that European performance is largely on a par with the United States and Japan (although Europe is behind when it comes to the other fundamental indicator, the ratio between investments in R&D and GDP). The real weakness lies in Europe's inability to transform European technological and scientific know-how, which is of a high standard, into effective opportunities. There are many ways in which we could try to improve co-operation between the world of research and the world of industry so as to stimulate the creation of new enterprises and consolidate existing ones in the innovative sectors with a high technological content (I am referring here not only to electronics and information technology, but also to biotechnology and life sciences). These are the sectors in which, as I have already said, advanced countries can maintain a competitive advantage over developing countries in the future.

(11) European small and medium-sized enterprises must grow *in both number and size*. To date, it is the first of these two aspects of growth that has received the greater attention in Europe. Assisting the creation of new enterprises is certainly very important, as they are breeding grounds for entrepreneurial skills and make a fundamental contribution to creating employment. Particularly in sectors requiring a high degree of innovation, they are a channel through which technological progress can fulfil all its potential. However, the creation of new enterprises is only part of the solution to the problem of boosting production. The establishment of many new businesses is offset by the failure of many others, and the net employment benefit is often less than expected. In reality there has to be a continual process of birth and growth. Small enterprises (or at least some of them) must become medium-sized and then large. This is the best guarantee that, over the long term, the

European economy will remain competitive in global markets of enormous magnitude. Probably not enough has been done to favour the growth of companies, although the situation differs a great deal from one country to another. According to a recent study reported in *Business Week*, of the 50 European companies with the highest rates of growth in the period 1991–6, 15 are located in Great Britain, 9 in Germany, 6 in France, 5 in Spain and only 4 in Italy. These differences between countries reflect various factors, but two must be strongly emphasized: (i) the *legislative framework*, with particular reference to its fiscal and employment components; (ii) the *efficiency of the financial markets*.

As far as the first aspect is concerned, many things are changing in our countries. In Italy, we are introducing ideas for a simpler and more equitable tax system and to help businesses with own-capital funding. We are also introducing changes to the labour market so that different types of employment (direct employment and self-employment) enjoy the same rights. In fact, we need to ensure adequate protection for all forms of work, while at the same time ensuring that businesses have sufficient flexibility in the way they manage human resources. We also have to devise different ways of taxing capital gains if we are to encourage the establishment and growth of businesses.

Efficient financial markets are also fundamental to helping companies grow in size. We have to ask ourselves in all honesty whether the accelerated growth that created companies of planetary size and significance in a few years could have happened here in Europe. The answer would have to be no, and I believe that the fundamental causes are lack of competition in the financial markets, not enough large-scale brokers, inadequate encouragement for growth in the tax system, too many currencies and fragmentation of the regulatory systems governing the markets.

In order to ensure a future for European industry, we need to change European finance. We have already made some progress with not insignificant international take-overs and mergers, but there have still been only a few large operations at international level that could significantly raise Europe's competitiveness. They are still being resisted and kept uneven by a residual sense of nationalism. Naturally, the largest enterprises will play an important role in consolidating the European oligopoly. If we look at the geographic distribution of the largest enterprises in the world, Europe's share is considerable, as I have previously pointed out. But if we put this into perspective, we will discover that there are actually two problems with large European enterprises: their capacity for growth (which is lower than that of the large American enterprises), and their sectorial specialization (which is more oriented towards traditional sectors than to the high-tech ones). As we know, more international competition implies many things for the economic systems of the industrialized countries, but above all *an enormous increase in the size of the market*.

In the second place, information technologies are encouraging research and innovation on an unprecedented scale. In many cases, although certainly not in all, this translates into an increase in the minimum size that enterprises must attain to sustain their related costs. Larger markets and higher overheads lead to greater concentration of capital, and, as has been said, European enterprises are too small. In many sectors they are becoming smaller in relative terms, because other parts of the world are creating enterprises of global dimensions more rapidly. It is, however, vital that we move in this direction, if Europe is to have companies capable of competing on the global markets in sectors with high degrees of research and development, as well as high degrees of economies of scale. To achieve this, we need first to make it easier for European companies to grow through mergers and take-overs. Although these have been bolstered in Europe, it is still behind the United States in terms of both the frequency and the size of such operations. In spite of all the progress that Europe has made with its financial markets, they are still excessively nationalistic in their orientation, and this, together with the legislative barriers I referred to earlier, is making it difficult for major take-overs and mergers across the borders of member states. Nevertheless, there have been some important new developments in Europe. I am thinking particularly of the *aerospace and defence electronics industries*, where action is being taken to promote restructuring and integration on a Europe-wide basis. I believe that this is an appropriate measure, given that the time of 'national rivalry' is over. We are now in a period of 'integrated projects', with all that entails in terms of mergers and take-overs, and individual countries will have to provide the necessary resources. It is particularly significant that this is occurring in the defence industry, as this field has long been dominated by national tradition. Once again we can draw a lesson from what is commonly called the real economy: EMU is in itself a powerful factor in harmonizing a country's collective structures. The euro impacts initially on purely monetary and financial matters, but ultimately on industrial matters as well.

I have looked in detail at company size, whether small, medium or large, but a final consideration must be the *major European networks*. We must regain the initiative, lost in the period after the Bangemann Report, for creating large networked infrastructures. From this perspective, Europe is falling significantly and worryingly behind in relation to the other principal regions of the world. The regions that were previously less developed are taking full advantage of being the last to arrive, and are setting up energy and telecommunications infrastructures based on the latest generation of technology. The United States is also developing powerful infrastructures, especially in the communications field, thanks to liberalization and the resulting competition. Europe, meanwhile, has come to a halt. It is certainly the case that the heavy budget restrictions imposed on member states and Community structures to meet convergence for the single currency contributed to this delay. However, now that monetary union has been achieved, the actual adjustment process will be rapid and effective in terms of production and employment, as long as it can rely on adequate networks. Communications, transport and energy are fundamental to the integration of production in the European Union. To achieve this, we need to overcome nationalistic attitudes (often reinforced by public ownership in the past or present) and rapidly integrate the public-service markets throughout Europe. The creation of large networked infrastructures should be placed in the wider context of the European Union's *enlargement towards the east*, which is the other fundamental objective that we set ourselves along with the single currency. We all know that the main communication lines have always run north–south. Now we need to develop the east–west ones. In fact we have physically to rebuild European

links that have been so important in the past. Europe's enlargement is a primary objective, particularly for Italy. Like Germany,
Italy is by its history and by its very nature drawn towards the
east, and it cannot shirk this challenge. It is a challenge that
will bring its share of changes and problems. These are countries
with income levels much lower than those of western European
countries. There will have to be changes to the agricultural
policy, the regional cohesion policies and other policies, but it
is a challenge that we, along with other Europeans, will have
to meet, in the belief that this is the new Europe.

(12) The EU's precious achievement of macroeconomic
stability is the starting-point for any proposals for economic or
industrial policies. Investment decisions can be sustained owing
to: (i) the substantial reduction in interest rates made possible
by the improvement in public accounts achieved by member
states in recent years; (ii) the further reductions still expected
in many countries; (iii) the massive flow of funds towards 'risk
capital' that has resulted from these prudent policies. Growth
will recover and be sustained partly because of the end of
macroeconomic uncertainty. What is more, a strong European
economy will also attract international capital and encourage
the transitional economies in eastern Europe to use it as an
instrument for international reserves. Strengthened by this
macroeconomic context, Europe has the opportunity to carry
through a series of microeconomic reforms to liberalize the
economy (particularly those sectors that are still protected)
and stimulate competition to the full. The way forward devised
many years ago for the Single Market has proved to be very
useful. Close examination shows it to have been a systematic and
ambitious supply-side economic project that aimed to remove
the rigidity in various markets and the barriers to mobility.
It gave rise to a period of economic growth in Europe and
improved business expectations that the Commission has
summarized as follows: increasing competition between manufacturing and service companies; a boost to the process of restructuring industry, which involved an explosion in the number
of mergers and take-overs; a reduction in prices, especially in
the public-service utilities through liberalization (I am referring
here to transport, financial services and telecommunications);

an increase in the EU's income of between 1.1 and 1.5 per cent over the period 1987–93; and greater cohesion between Europe's different regions.[10]

We have to continue down this road, pushing the reform process further towards a 'lean state', a compatible welfare state, and a labour market in which there is equality of opportunity for all. It is a market in which competition fulfils all its potential, with the completion of the privatization process (so important for creating new economic players) and the removal of any remaining monopoly positions.

(13) Now that we have successfully launched the adventure of the single currency, we should not forget the lesson of our founding fathers. Europe, which has become a leading player in the world economy, grew out of a political project. The economic successes, of which we can be justly proud and whose most significant stages I have reviewed, should be seen as an integral part of a vision that has always had political integration as its ultimate objective. Today this extraordinary intuition has lost none of its vitality, and we intend to use its inspiration in our daily political activities. Besides, what would be the sense in bringing our currencies together, if this were not part of a project to strengthen our common policies in all sectors? This commitment has been made all the more pressing by the twin challenge of enlargement and the 'demand for Europe' coming from such disparate regions as the Mediterranean, the Balkans, Asia and Latin America, not to mention Africa. Our response to all these partners must be an energetic one, and be perceived as such. People on the outside no longer understand how a European Union that can create a currency capable of taking on the role of reserve currency for sovereign states, and becoming a vehicle for international payments, is not able at the same time to come up with a common foreign policy. Too often, even in the recent past, international tensions and regional crises, some of which occurred at our very door, have revealed our difficulty in presenting the political face of Europe, a continent that symbolizes democracy and affluence. Our humanitarian commitment, of which we are justly proud, is all too rarely accompanied by the ability to play the active political role that is required of us. Europe was born from a project that is open

to the world and is alien to all 'fortress' mentalities or barriers that divide us from the outside and lead to conflicts between civilizations. Our own history has been forged through the meeting of cultures capable of assimilating different contributions and entering into dialogue with adjacent regions. Our vision of international competition is inspired by co-operation and the reconciliation of conflicting interests. It is a vision that categorically rejects conflict. For these reasons, the demand for Europe cannot go unheeded. We owe it to our citizens, who would not understand it if Europe were reduced to a mere head on a coin, and we owe it to all those beyond our borders who look to our progress for hope and encouragement.

Notes

1   The reader is referred in particular to the analysis in ch. 4.
2   The effects of the law on corporate governance, called the Draghi Law from the name of the politician who drafted it, included Olivetti's raid on Telecom Italia, which, leaving aside any judgement on its wisdom, represents the most spectacular example of how companies and markets have become open to attack.
3   *The World in 2020: Toward a New Global Age* (Paris: OECD, 1997).
4   For reasons of uniformity, the calculations were made by OECD researchers with reference to GDP values in dollars for 1992 and using exchanges rates at 'purchasing power parity'.
5   Although this list is far from exhaustive, some of the relevant titles are: M. Albert, *Capitalism Against Capitalism* (London: Whurr Publishers, 1998); R. Dahrendorf, 'Economic opportunity, civil society and political liberty' (paper presented to the conference held on 11–12 March 1995 in Copenhagen on *Rethinking Social Development*); R. Dore, *Taking Japan Seriously* (London: Athlone Press, 1987); L. Thurow, *Head to Head: the Coming Economic Battle Among Japan, Europe and America* (London: Allen & Unwin, 1993).
6   M. L. Dertouzos, R. K. Lester and R. M. Solow, *Made in America* (Milan: Comunità, 1991).
7   The Institute for Prospective Technological Studies (IPTS) Report, Special Issue, *Made in Europe* (Seville: June 1997).
8   Eurostat, *Les Entreprises en Europe: quatrième rapport* (Brussels: 1996).
9   European Commission, *Panorama of EU Industry '97* (Brussels).
10 Ibid.

9

The economy and the technological position of European industry

(1) The 'age of the Euro', which formally commenced on 1 January 1999, could be approached from several angles. The first is an explicitly *political* perspective. At the beginning of the twenty-first century, it is the coin rather the sword that symbolizes sovereignty. It took a political decision by eleven different states to give it up, and this represents a further step along the extraordinary road to European integration. I believe that the single currency will generate other forms of solidarity that will go far beyond the economic and monetary sphere. It is important to remember that such a decision has never been taken before in history. In the past, the loss of monetary sovereignty has always been the result of wars and military conquests.

The second perspective is *macroeconomic*, and this is the one that has received most attention until now. In the wake of the Maastricht Treaty, convergence between the countries participating in Economic and Monetary Union has helped create a 'culture of stability' in Europe. Historical experience shows that low interest rates constitute the first step towards lasting economic growth. A long-term policy to combat unemployment can only be based on this kind of growth. Even though the lead-up to the euro may have caused a temporary slowdown in growth, the positive effects are destined to prevail in the long term.

The third perspective that we are to examine, the *microeconomic* one, deserves attention in this connection. The microeconomic perspective relates to the competitiveness and productivity of companies operating in the euro zone. As integration gathers pace with the birth of the single currency, global competition is forcing Europe to rationalize, and this process is not yet complete.

(2) The creation of the Common Market and the European Union, on the road to the formation of a single Europe-wide market, has already done much to encourage restructuring in European industry. In the early days, when national markets were dominant but wider competition was already forecast, there was a great wave of mergers around Europe. Their form was unexpected, but entirely understandable from a rational point of view. In a period when policies were still national, but a loss of the state's power of intervention was clearly inevitable, every government hurried to strengthen its own enterprises so they could face up to future international competition more effectively. In the first period of the European Common Market therefore, corporate mergers and take-overs were mainly national.

During this period – the 1960s – leading national companies reinforced, rather than reduced, the national character of European industry. In the iron and steel, chemical and car industries and in all sectors where there were very few manufacturers, industrial concentration increased within each country. In fact for many years, mergers between firms in different European countries were very limited (the one between Agfa and Gevaert was the only real example). Paradoxically the turbulent pre-war years, which were plagued by nationalism, witnessed the creation of some large multinational companies (for example Royal Dutch, Shell and Unilever), while the first period of united Europe was one of increased industrial nationalism. The countries that joined the concentration process late (including Italy, partly because it had a very large number of publicly owned companies) found themselves in a markedly weak position in terms of market strength compared with those countries whose companies had already gone through the merger phase.

When the new economic Europe had consolidated itself and started to harmonize its administrative and competition rules, it entered a new phase in which companies adopted Europe-wide strategies and thought with the logic of a Europe-wide market. International mergers were carried through, and companies implemented strategies that minimized costs while insuring against the risk of monetary devaluation. In this period, even the more peripheral countries were involved in the process of capital concentration and had policies to encourage the localization of industries. For example, the Spanish manufacturing base of its motor car industry developed in this manner.

We now find ourselves in a new phase, the *final* one, which aims to create a single market with rules tending towards unification and with a single currency. This phase will probably lead steadily towards a level of concentration of oligopolistic industries comparable with that of the United States. The number of motor car, chemical and electronics manufacturers is still far higher in Europe than in the United States.

The three perspectives just outlined – the political, the macroeconomic and the microeconomic – all have great importance, and they have been widely discussed in previous chapters. Here I will give further attention to the microeconomic perspective. Once macroeconomic convergence has been achieved, this perspective will be increasingly crucial, although it has been stubbornly ignored in political and economic analyses of the euro.

(3) First there is what I call 'shuffling the cards' of European industry. There have been numerous mergers and take-overs, particularly in the second half of 1998.[1] It is difficult to say whether or not these were related to the birth of the euro, but there can be no doubt that European industrial structures are in ferment. There has been a great deal of activity in connection with American companies: for example the merger between Daimler-Benz and Chrysler, the Deutsche Bank take-over of Bankers Trust (which created the largest financial services group in the world) and even the merger between Ford and Volvo.

There is also considerable dynamism within European industry: apart from the previously mentioned merger between British Aerospace and GEC Marconi, there have been the cases of Hoechst-Rhône Poulenc (pharmaceuticals and agrochemicals), Zeneca-Astra (pharmaceuticals), Viag-Alusuisse (aluminium and packaging), and Total-Petrofina (oil industry), to say nothing of the innumerable mergers in the banking and insurance sector.[2] This wave of mergers and take-overs is far from over. Indeed it has only just begun, given that one merger creating a dominant company usually leads to another that can compete in terms of industrial power and financial strength.

Generally speaking, the purpose of most agreements *between European companies* (the absolute majority of agreements in recent years) is to achieve the necessary size to compete at international level. They can be looked on favourably because, with the globalization of markets, they often produce high levels of efficiency without reducing competition. It is possible that there will be some kind of reaction in the future, if this process continues to be led (and perhaps dominated) by German companies. Although it is very difficult, for institutional and structural reasons, for companies from other countries taking over German ones, the greater dynamism of the latter does not yet appear to have worried European business and governments.

(4) These examples demonstrate that, although the cards will be shuffled on a vast scale, some sectors of European industry will be more affected by change than others. I am thinking of the aerospace industries and the 'life sciences', but also of air transport, defence, railway construction and, of course, telecommunications and information technologies. Technological factors undoubtedly lie at the root of current changes in these fundamental sectors. But clearly there are also compelling institutional reasons, such as privatization and liberalization policies.[3] This is true not only of sectors traditionally subject to competition, but also of those that have so far been immune to it. Indeed these changes have started in the defence industry, where the attainment of economies of scale and advanced technology has been obstructed by the predominantly national context in which the supply and demand of military hardware operate. Privatization and liberalization are helping create new larger enterprises capable of operating beyond national borders and sustaining the expected rates of growth.

(5) We owe a large part of the institutional and structural changes of recent years to what I have always called the 'Europe

factor'. Examples are the Single European Act of 1987 and even the previous White Paper of 1985, for which Jacques Delors campaigned strongly. Not only were the foundations laid for the Single Market with complete freedom of circulation of goods, services, persons and capital, but the 'rules of the game' also started to become more competitive. For example, the merger rules of 1989 banned 'state assistance', and the drive for liberalization and privatization particularly affected those sectors that had previously been regulated on a national basis and were dominated by national monopolies. The break with national monopolies led to the emergence of large enterprises that were no longer restricted to local business, and were therefore capable of becoming cores around which to consolidate industrial and service activity.

(6) The current industrial reorganization is mainly due to the vitality of large groups. As has already been shown,[4] many of them are important public-service management enterprises or producers of goods subject entirely to public demand, and were created by privatizations during the 1990s or are undergoing privatization. Equally they could be the great and glorious multidivisional electronics and engineering groups, like GEC, Daimler, Ansaldo, Breda or Siemens, that run an entire range of businesses, including industrial complexes for producing energy, electric motors, electric trains, rolling-stock, armaments and aeronautics.

For all these new players, the fundamental and critical resource is the ability to maintain and develop control over production technologies and research and development centres. The European input into the teaching of theoretical and applied science is not enough for our continent to fulfil the role that we expect of it in determining the future of our planet. The degree of our commitment to research programmes will be one of the most important testing grounds in the years to come.

(7) Technological competition, as a result of the challenges it poses, requires extra attention and increased resources from all European countries. This is particularly true for some countries that have so far done little to renew theoretical and applied research structures in Europe. Italy, which spends only 1.1 per

cent of GDP on R&D, and Spain, which spends 0.8–0.9 per
cent, are examples of this inadequacy. The average for OECD
countries is 2.2 per cent, and for the EU it is 1.9 per cent.[5]
There are cultural and historical reasons for falling so far behind,
but the problem must be confronted head-on as the principal
enemy of our future development. We must treat it as an urgent
priority that concerns the relationship between the whole of
Europe and the United States and between some European
countries and others. It is a more universal and pervasive problem than is generally imagined. It concerns the future independence of our continent and affects the most sensitive aspects
of our development.

This has many implications, the first of which concerns
defence. On this point, suffice it to recall that the gap between
Europe and the United States in the most modern military
technologies has become so wide that it has even made joint
military operations difficult. The technological differences
between our defence industry are so marked that, in plain language, it has become difficult *to speak and to act together*, even
when there is a will to do so.

As far as the most sensitive aspects of development are concerned, the life sciences and information and communications
technologies are now becoming fundamental for all other industrial sectors. If we are weak today in these two sectors, we
will be weak tomorrow in all industries, all services and even
the civil service. Europe is weak precisely in these sectors, and
Italy is in a particularly weak situation compared with the other
European countries.[6] It would take too long here to analyse
in detail our educational system and our research organization
in both the public and private sectors. I will simply stress the
need for a veritable qualitative and quantitative revolution in
this sphere in an extremely short period of time.

The creation of the euro, which above all means totally
fixed exchange rates between the countries involved, tends to
concentrate production where it is cheapest, and research activities in the areas where there is the greatest supply of high-
quality researchers. While we see the single currency as a sign
of hope, we also know that it could lead to the concentration
of industrial activity and this would reverse the decentralization
that the European project has so far generated. What is more,

unless we understand the seriousness of this danger and take swift remedial action, we will have an increasing gap between the regions and countries in which people invent and design and the regions and countries in which people apply what others have invented and designed. Currently there does not seem to be sufficient awareness of this risk in Mediterranean countries. Little attention is being given to its implications for the quantitative and qualitative development of our society. It is time to act in the knowledge that, even if we started our Copernican revolution today, we would not see its fruits for many years, the years necessary to provide new human resources.

(8) Fortunately, technological development is not restricted to the sectors I have mentioned, although it is very much affected by them. European industry contains an endless wealth of sectors and sub-sectors in which a vast network of small and medium-sized enterprises maintains the level of innovation, just as much as the large enterprises. Even in these cases, however, innovation in any one sector tends to progress more rapidly where there is the greatest number of enterprises concentrated in a region. In other words, there is a centre and a periphery for sectors as well. So our regional industrial policies must be sensitive to these characteristics of the technological development of small and medium-sized enterprises. Indeed, where the fabric of industry is made up of SMEs that typically do not have research and development laboratories at their disposal or only have laboratories with very limited resources and functions, innovation and technological development are linked to interaction between several parties. These vary from large public research centres and universities to small innovative companies, and centres for applied research, vocational training, services and experimentation.

The concept of technological transfer has to be substantially revised within this context. The idea of 'drives' to persuade small businesses to adopt innovative technologies is no longer practical. We must develop systems of relations, exchanges of information, the movement of skilled workers and liaison between international centres of excellence so as to encourage companies to take innovative decisions. In recent years, the

European policy on this subject has been radically changed: the concept of research and development (R&D) is no longer associated solely with large industrial organizations, but has been extended to the whole world of production and services. All the recent EU documents and programmes, from the Green Paper on Innovation to the Fifth Framework Programme,[7] are finally prioritizing closer relations between R&D and small and medium-sized enterprises, in order to make research results available to the latter.

(9) To enable small businesses to play their part, we have to recognize the way the market generates innovation by showing which needs have to be resolved, as we are currently doing with the Fifth Framework Programme.[8] Not surprisingly, the main proposals of this programme (the so-called 'key actions') take into account the crucial issues concerning the future of European society and the world: quality of life, sustainable growth, the information society, energy and the environment. These are accompanied by horizontal programmes, the most significant of which concern the involvement of SMEs and the improvement of human potential. On this point, we have to pay particular attention to Europe's position *vis-à-vis* its competitors in the high-tech sectors. It is unarguably a position of weakness, if we look only at the large-scale high-tech sectors (electronics, information technology and biotechnology), where there can be no doubt about the greater strength of the Americans and the Japanese, and their joint domination of international trade.

However, new areas could be opened up to European industry. While today the United States dominates the vast science-based industries, Europe has considerable advantages in sectors requiring a specialized workforce, in which human resources and their accumulated experience and skills take on an important role at the upper and intermediate levels of the management organization. While Europe's share of the world market for the science-based sectors, after deducting intra-European trade, is about 18 per cent, its share of the skill-based sectors is close to 31 per cent. This might appear a small consolation for our great weakness in sectors with a high degree of research and development. But it is not so small in terms of industrial strength. For a country's balance of trade, it is very important to be able to manufacture specialized producer goods, luxury shoes or luxury cars efficiently. However, our share in the production of these goods is being increasingly eroded by international competition (especially from the developing countries), and, particularly over the long term, many of these sectors will be revolutionized by radical changes induced by new lines of research.

Finally, the EU's Fifth Framework Programme identifies high-quality services for individuals or the public as new positive elements. Innovation based largely on demand will be genuinely encouraged in a Europe that attributes increasing value to matters relating to the quality of life: health, the environment and transport systems, to mention just a few examples. These needs, so strongly expressed by advanced societies, are stimulating innovative developments in large and small European enterprises. At the same time, the research undertaken in response to these needs can generate technological spin-offs for other sectors just as the defence industry and defence-related research have done in the past. New room for activity and employment also lies in this direction.

(10) In the age of the euro, macroeconomic stability and the disappearance of exchange-rate fluctuations are radically changing the context in which our companies operate. The euro will enormously increase competition between companies in Europe. In the judgement of many observers, the three areas most affected by the introduction of the single currency are pricing policies (which will become more transparent and comparable with other countries), relations with suppliers and the internal structures of companies. Overall, the euro will bring benefits and profits to many companies, and provide them with great opportunities to simplify and rationalize their operations. But not all companies will be rewarded by the new competitive regime: only the well-managed ones will benefit. The same will be true of nations and countries, although on a larger scale. The euro makes the adjustments produced by currency fluctuations impossible. It tends to make Europe's strong points more competitive. It tends to make the competition more bitter between the various 'national systems'. These transitions, which

will certainly be difficult, are, however, necessary if only to maintain our position in the world as globalization proceeds. In spite of all the problems it obviously creates, the euro is the instrument of our future survival. It is up to us to devise appropriate policies to make good use of our human resources, so that Europe's peripheries, as well as the centre, can play their part in this great task.

Notes

1 In 1998 the next wave of mergers and take-overs, which had been growing since the middle of the decade, reached its highest level, with transactions covering 2,400 billion dollars, a 50% increase on the previous year (see the figures published by the Securities Data Company, from which it can be seen that two-thirds of the merger activity concerned American companies).

2 Any list of mergers and take-overs would run the risk of being overtaken by events in a very short time. Not a day goes by without the announcement of large-scale mergers, take-overs, grand alliances, joint ventures, and even hostile take-over bids in one European country or another.

3 Cf. P. Bianchi, *L'industria europea nell'età dell'euro*, report submitted to the Thirty-ninth Annual Scientific Meeting of the Italian Society of Economists, Milan, Catholic University of the Sacred Heart, 22 October 1998 (typescript).

4 Ibid.

5 The data refers to 1995 or 1996, and is taken from the recent OECD publication *Sciences, Technology and Industry Outlook 1998* (Paris).

6 The ninth CER–IRS report on Italian industry and industrial policy gives a wide-ranging and well-documented evaluation of Italian industry's 'weak points' (failure to use the skilled workforce, insufficient scientific and applied research activity, and under-representation in the more innovative sectors of the economy): *Competitività e regolazione: ripensare il governo dell'economia a un passo dall'euro* (Bologna: Il Mulino, 1998); see in particular the introduction and ch. 1, pp. 11–105).

7 The Fifth Framework Programme is an initiative over several years (1998–2002) that provides a single programmatic and financial framework for the Community's action on technological research and development. The programme, formally adopted by the Research Council on 22 December 1998, has a total budget

of 14.96 billion euros (of which 1.26 billion euros is allocated to Euratom programmes). The Research Council has also drawn up specific programmes for which the overall programme has arranged invitations to tender, to be published in the Official Journal of the European Community.

8   See *Fifth Framework Programme for Technological Research and Development* (Brussels: EU Commission working paper, November 1997).

10

Employment in Europe

(1) Having achieved the criteria set by the Maastricht Treaty for admission to Economic and Monetary Union, most European countries, including Italy, found themselves facing very high unemployment levels, averaging 11 per cent for the European Union as a whole.[1] European unemployment is not only high and persistent as an *aggregate* figure, but it is also very *heterogeneous* if the distribution is broken down by geographic area, educational qualifications and age group.

(2) I fully share the view that today unemployment is the greatest challenge facing the EU. The task of fighting unemployment is made all the more difficult in our affluent societies by our ability to sustain a high number of unemployed through welfare provisions and parental assistance, while low-paid jobs go to workers from outside the European Union. More generally, Western industrialized economies are facing increasing globalization which brings with it a continual and radical change in the composition of world production. The production of skill-intensive goods is acquiring increasing importance in OECD countries, as a result of the greater international division of labour, and there is a relative decline in the sectors producing labour-intensive goods. It is now a priority to make our economies, or rather our workforces, capable of dealing with this changed international division of labour. Leaving aside this new situation in the world economy, I want to look more closely at European unemployment.

(3) Broadly speaking, economists support two different theories to explain the persistence of high unemployment in the EU.

(i) Many European scholars claim that the best way to achieve permanent employment and perhaps growth in GDP is to implement 'structural' reforms, such as reforms to the labour market and the welfare state. By making it easier and less costly to recruit and dismiss employees, enterprises should be encouraged to take on new staff or at least be more inclined to take them on. 'Making work pay', to use the title of a well-known OECD study into unemployment benefits,[2] is supposed to increase the work incentive and reduce the burden of welfare costs to be borne by the working population. Some economists, also of this school of thought, argue the need for a reduction in income tax and other forms of taxation on work, even in the absence of a corresponding reduction in welfare services. These 'fiscal depreciations' involve reductions in welfare contributions and increases in indirect taxation (or even in direct taxation, as this leads to an increase in the progressiveness of taxation).

(ii) The other school of thought is that the increase in European unemployment is mainly attributable to over-restrictive demand-management policies. Unemployment will be reabsorbed once economic recovery has gained momentum. The fundamental argument is that an excessively monetary policy over the whole of the last decade is the principal cause of the lack of growth and the failure to create new jobs. Governments should therefore adopt policies for stimulating demand and, above all, investment. According to the recent *Manifesto contro la disoccupazione nell'Unione europea* of a group of scholars led by Franco Modigliani,[3] the principal cause of European unemployment is the decline in the rate of investment over the last decade. A reversal in this investment trend could therefore solve our unemployment problem, just as implementing policies, including monetary policy, more suited to the European dimension could stimulate a new accumulation of capital.

I am aware that the Modigliani *Manifesto* deals both with demand-side policies (the revival of overall demand) and supply-side policies (the reform of labour, goods and service markets, as well as unemployment benefit systems). I am equally aware of the emphasis that the authors repeatedly place on the 'complementary nature' of the various measures. Nevertheless, it seems to me that aggregate demand-side policies (growth in demand based on a strong recovery in the investment rate) have been the most innovative contribution to the recent debate and are the distinguishing features of this *Manifesto*, which is of a clearly reformist nature.

(4) The fact is that significant changes have taken place in Europe over the last decade, not only in the tone of macroeconomic policies, but also in the institutions that regulate the labour market. The two diametrically opposed theories I have just outlined do not always take account of this. Some reforms were made in our labour market as least as far back as the mid-1980s. Many countries have become more selective in their unemployment benefits, while others have made the regulations protecting employment rights less strict, and have allowed greater flexibility in agreements on working time. Countries such as Holland and Sweden have amended their tax systems, shifting some taxation from the cost of labour to general taxation, albeit within an unchanged or only slightly lower indirect cost of labour.

Changes have more frequently been made to the methods by which existing regulations are enforced. In particular, more rigid criteria have been introduced for paying unemployment benefit, and checks have even been carried out on people's real availability for work. It would therefore be misleading to regard European labour market regulation as completely unchanged since the oil crises of 1973 and 1979.

(5) On the other hand, these reforms have all been of an 'incremental' and marginal nature. In other words, they have not pulled out the old regulations by their roots, but have simply added other more liberal ones (in practice, these are new types of contract). The changes are also restricted to just a few segments of the labour market (for example, the young) or directed at those who work in regions with high unemployment rates or who have few chances of re-entering the world of work. Moreover, the cuts in unemployment benefits have never been dramatic never having exceeded 5–10 per cent.

Consequently, the reforms have often ended up increasing the 'dualism' and institutional complexity of European labour markets. Questions about the distribution of income are always central to the great European unemployment problem and this is even truer now than it was about ten years ago. In conclusion, these reforms, precisely because of their marginal nature, have hardly been perceived as real changes.

(6) I am quite convinced that European unemployment is not a problem that can be resolved *exclusively* either by a reduction in interest rates or by macroeconomic policies. Instead what is required is interaction between policies and a mix of both macroeconomic and microeconomic policies.[4] A renewed job-creation programme in Europe must therefore be founded on solid macroeconomic stability, which is a basic prerequisite for prolonged economic growth. At the same time, we must learn lessons from both the successes and failures experienced by European countries that can boast a history of structural reforms in this field.

(7) More than anything else, Economic and Monetary Union is an act of faith in Europe. The creation of the euro is an unprecedented event in the history of the world.[5] The process that led to monetary union under the Maastricht Treaty produced considerable results in the fight against inflation and excessive budget deficits. The macroeconomic convergence (price stability, public finances in order, exchange-rate stability, and convergence towards a lower threshold of long-term interest rates) outperformed even the most optimistic expectations. As we can see from numerous experiences around the world, and especially the United States in the 1990s, defeating inflation and putting the public finances in order must be considered a great success and a precondition for effectively combating unemployment. This has now been achieved by all the members of the European Union, including Italy.

The most visible result of this macroeconomic stabilization has been a drastic reduction in interest rates, especially in certain countries. Both large and small investors benefit from this, and investment has always represented the real engine of economic growth. During the 1980s and 1990s, high real interest rates in many European countries contributed to Europe's increasing unemployment. Today, European countries must keep faith with a policy of low interest rates. In terms of budget policy, this implies commitment to upholding the Stability and Growth Pact. If we keep to the Pact, we will be able to signal to the markets our commitment to fiscal discipline over the long term, without obstructing any appropriate policy to reduce the tax burden.

Support for the accumulation of capital and support for fiscal discipline are not incompatible. The launch of the single currency also means that centralized management of currency reserves is taken over by the European Central Bank and relinquished by each of the central banks. Not all the available international reserves have been transferred. About 50 per cent has remained in the liquidity of national banks, given that there is now much less need to intervene in the markets. The national banks could gradually alter the composition of their currency portfolios. They could slowly shift in a manner that would not impede the euro's exchange-rate policy as pursued by the European Central Bank, from investments in securities in dollars or yen to long-term bond securities issued by the European Investment Bank (EIB). With these funds, the EIB could finance private projects to set up a European network of public utilities. These services would be franchised to private operators for the appropriate number of years.

(8) Returning to microeconomic policies, there are, as I have already said, some positive lessons to be learnt from OECD countries in the field of structural reforms. One thing is certain: the current situation no longer permits policies that fail to give due consideration to political feasibility. Even academics now seem totally aware of this. I wish to stress that a proper definition of the context in which microeconomic policy operates must include not only the necessary reform of the labour, goods, services and capital markets, but also other elements of what is usually called the 'national system'. I am referring here to the educational system, workforce training, public and private scientific research centres, and the development of the new information society. To put it in a nutshell, I still believe that education is the foundation of all wealth.[6] Hence Europe must raise the technological level of its production by investing greater resources in research and development, and improving links

between universities and companies. Europe must put more emphasis on the centrality of its technical colleges, its high-level professional training, and the continuous training and retraining of its workforce. Europe must go on helping small and medium-sized enterprises to get started by giving them tax breaks and genuine incentives.[7] Europe, as a whole, seems to have lost its excellence in technical instruction, although the system of technical colleges in Germany (the deservedly famous *Fachhochschulen*) works very well. I believe that it is no accident that Germany has kept a strong manufacturing base in its economy.

For a few years now, there has been a debate in Europe on how small and medium-sized enterprises (SMEs) and business parks, which are so widespread in Italy, manage to reconcile three things that do not easily develop together: business efficiency, the creation of new jobs, and social cohesion. The Italian tradition in this field is based on a series of factors that facilitate localization of industry by drawing companies into a given area.[8] But 'human resources' have always been, and still are, of the greatest importance.

The new policies that Italy has been implementing for a few years have been consistent with this tradition of diffuse business activity. There are, for instance, policies that aim to twin business parks in the north-east with areas in the south, to identify sites in the south where tax incentives, more flexible regulations for the labour market, and communications infrastructures could help new businesses to start up. There are also schemes that offer loans to help young, potential small-business people to get started.

(9) The return of the Mediterranean's centrality, which I have already discussed in detail, throws new light on the potential of Italy's south – the Mezzogiorno – which can truly claim to be the gateway to Europe, and, in another way, to be the 'new frontier' of our country. The phase of economic growth that I am certain EMU will bring must not simply saturate northern Italy's industrial capacity, as has occurred in the past. Given this phase of growth, we must grasp the opportunity to bring into play the great latent resources of the south. For the first time since Italian Unification, we are entering a phase in which

the Mezzogiorno can play its part in the development of both Italy and Europe, as an area where our industrial base can grow rapidly. It is no longer the South simply as a market outlet or the South as an opportunity to obtain funding and incentives to attract northern businessmen. Many parts of our country's business community have gradually become convinced that the Mezzogiorno has enormous development potential, and therefore represents a real opportunity.

We are well aware that everywhere work has to be created by companies. The idea that state intervention is capable of replacing private enterprise has gone forever. Today, many companies look to the Mezzogiorno, but they require specific conditions, which it is the business of national and local government to provide. Such conditions have to make investment in the Mezzogiorno advantageous. I have always seen four conditions as a priority, and I concentrated all my efforts on these during the period I was in government. These are the fight against crime and the recovery of the state's control over the territory, greater efficiency in the civil service which must become a support and not an obstruction to enterprise, modernization of infrastructures and better-quality council services, and greater flexibility and lower labour costs.

I believe that it is right to proceed in these four directions, adopting an approach that we could call the 'development of variety'. This would recognize that today we no longer have a single Mezzogiorno, but many distinct realities. It follows that we no longer need a rigid and uniform model of development, but specific and differentiated measures that start in the areas with the greatest potential for development and the greatest aptitude.

Creating new jobs in the Mezzogiorno is an ambiguous and empty promise if it is not made clear that this is 'real work'. Of course, we can fund temporary activities, invest in 'work experience' schemes for young people, and accompany welfare payments with requests that those receiving them be available for socially useful work. But these measures on their own engender passivity but not hope or development. Real jobs require the presence of businesses. They can be small or large enterprises, craft industries or co-operatives, as long as they have the will to survive in the market. Our problem is thus how to arouse local enthusiasm and attract capital. There is now competition to obtain not subsidies but investments. This implies a strong public commitment to guaranteeing legality, improving education and creating an adequate network of services. But the Mezzogiorno becomes an 'opportunity' if, at least initially, we can reduce costs, including labour costs. We have ended the bureaucratic monopoly over recruitment, and we have facilitated part-time, temporary employment and training contracts. All of this is helping us along this new course.

(10) To sum up, effective European action on employment requires both wisdom and courage. We need to be able to bring four strategies together. First of all, we must ensure, as a precondition, that the economy continues to grow steadily. Second, we need to complete the market reforms in order to match labour supply and demand more closely. Third, we have to distribute available work better, using shorter hours in exchange for flexibility, part-time and temporary work. Finally, we need to push ahead resolutely with training the workforce.

All this would bring unemployment down considerably. But, if we are to attain full employment, we need to mobilize resources on a massive scale to create many more new enterprises and jobs than can be ensured by any economic recovery. I must confess that I had expected the launch of EMU to be sustained by greater growth, but the current situation in the world probably does not allow it. Although Europe is working, Europeans are aware of the risk in this new phase and 'Europhoria' appears to be waning.

But a negative economic situation will not change things. Even in this period of crisis and before it formally came into existence, EMU has shown that it can work. Perhaps the very difficulties that we experienced at the outset will drive us towards greater co-ordination over economic policy. This was precisely the intention of those who boldly went ahead with the launch of EMU and the single currency, looking forward to the day when Europe will indeed be ready for political union.

Notes

1 This (average) European unemployment rate, which reached high points of between 15 and 20%, contrasts markedly with the American performance. The unemployment rate in the United States fell at the beginning of 1998 to about 4.3–4.4% (see *Economic Report of the President* quoted in *ECB Monthly Bulletin*). A figure similar to the American one has also been recorded in Japan, although the labour market there operates in significantly and fundamentally different ways.

2 *Employment Outlook* (Paris: 1997); *Making Work Pay: Taxation, Benefits, Employment and Unemployment* (Paris: OECD, 1997).

3 F. Modigliani, J. P. Fitoussi, B. Moro, D. Snower, R. Solow, A. Steinherr, P. Sylos Labini, *Manifesto contro la disoccupazione nell'Unione europea* (1998).

4 For an in-depth study of the right sequence in which to co-ordinate the two major policies available to governments (macro-economic policies to stimulate growth and structural reforms of the labour, goods and service markets), and for some possible scenarios with reference to Germany, France and Italy, see I. Visco, 'Economic growth and European unemployment', paper presented to the Tri-Nation Conference, Monaco, 14 October 1998 (Paris: OECD, typescript).

5 EMU, its historical and economic profile, and its implications for the European economy have been widely discussed in previous chapters. See in particular chs 1 and 4.

6 Starting with the works of Paul Romer in the 1980s, the new theories on 'endogenous growth' have the merit of presenting a vision of the economy in which the accumulation of 'knowledge' and not just physical capital governs long-term growth. New knowledge, in turn, is the product of scientific and technological research and workforce training. For a reference to this debate and its policy implications, see R. Prodi and F. Mosconi, *Istituzioni economiche, istituzioni politiche* (Bologna: Il Mulino, 1995), pp. 1073–87.

7 For a full discussion of America's technological leadership in all the high-tech industries and high levels of research, see ch. 8.

8 It is mainly because of these characteristics that the Italian experience of large SME networks and business parks has for some years been regularly cited as a model of job creation in the conclusions to all the most important international summits (from the G7 and G8 summits to the European Councils). It is also frequently taken as a model by newly industrialized countries (from India to Latin America), when undertaking economic reforms.